One Faith, Two Authorities

In the series *Religious Engagement in Democratic Politics*, edited by Paul A. Djupe

ALSO IN THE SERIES

Paul A. Djupe and Ryan L. Claassen, ed., *The Evangelical Crackup? The Future of the Evangelical-Republican Coalition*

One Faith, Two Authorities

Tension between Female Religious and Male Clergy in the American Catholic Church

Jeanine E. Kraybill

TEMPLE UNIVERSITY PRESS
Philadelphia • Rome • Tokyo

TEMPLE UNIVERSITY PRESS
Philadelphia, Pennsylvania 19122
tupress.temple.edu

Published 2019

Some information in chapter 2 is also noted in "Non-Ordained: Examining the Level of Female Religious Political Engagement & Social Policy Influence within the American Catholic Church." *Journal of Fieldwork in Religion* 11, no. 2 (2016): 137–156. Some information from chapters 3 and 4 is noted in "Evaluating Policy Differences Between Male and Female Religious Groups: A Study of the Social Policy Statements by the United States Conference of Catholic Bishops and the Leadership Conference of Women Religious." *The Journal of Communication and Religion* 39, no. 3 (Fall 2016): 76–99.

Library of Congress Cataloging-in-Publication Data

Names: Kraybill, Jeanine E., author.
Title: One faith, two authorities : tension between female religious and male clergy in the American Catholic Church / Jeanine E. Kraybill.
Description: Philadelphia : Temple University Press, 2019. | Series: Religious engagement in democratic politics | Includes bibliographical references and index. |
Identifiers: LCCN 2018030493 (print) | LCCN 2018046232 (ebook) | ISBN 9781439913833 (E-Book) | ISBN 9781439913819 (cloth : alk. paper) | ISBN 9781439913826 (pbk. : alk. paper)
Subjects: LCSH: Women in church work—United States. | Man-woman relationships—United States—Religious aspects—Catholic Church. | Catholic Church—United States—Clergy—Attitudes. | Christian leadership—United States—Catholic Church. | Laity—United States—Catholic Church—Attitudes. | Christianity and politics—Catholic Church.
Classification: LCC BX1407.W65 (ebook) | LCC BX1407.W65 K73 2019 (print) | DDC 282/.73082—dc23
LC record available at https://lccn.loc.gov/2018030493

♾ The paper used in this publication meets the requirements of the American National Standard for Information Sciences—Permanence of Paper for Printed Library Materials, ANSI Z39.48-1992

Printed in the United States of America

9 8 7 6 5 4 3 2 1

For my goddaughters:

Riley, Sofia, and Opal

Contents

Acknowledgments

I would like to acknowledge the work of Catholic female religious and clergy who dedicate their lives to the service of others, especially the female religious who educated me, my sisters, and generations of young women. I would also like to express my sincere gratitude to the individuals who supported my journey with this project and have been major influences in my academic career. In particular, I thank Paul Djupe, Jennifer Merolla, Jean Schroedel, and John Moore for their invaluable mentorship, along with my colleagues Raul Madrid Jr., Ariana Moreno, Randy Villages, and Chris Baarstad. Furthermore, I am thankful to California State University, Bakersfield, the School of Social Sciences and Education, and my dear colleagues in the Department of Political Science for their support. Last, I thank my own family, especially my parents, Michael and Lisa DiCesaris, and siblings, Michael, Jennifer, and Juleen, who are a continuous source of faith and encouragement. Most important, I sincerely thank my dear husband, Jesse Kraybill for his friendship, love, and unwavering support and belief in me.

One Faith, Two Authorities

1

Introduction

"Bishop Explains Vatican's Criticism of U.S. Nuns" (NPR 2012b); "A War on Nuns?"; "Vatican Reprimands U.S. Nuns Group" (Goodstein 2012)—in the spring of 2012 media headlines across the country brought attention to the Vatican's Congregation for the Doctrine of the Faith's (CDF) issuance of a formal Doctrinal Assessment of the Leadership Conference of Women Religious (LCWR), an association of female religious congregational leaders who represent 80 percent of the fifty-seven thousand nuns in the United States (LCWR 2017a). "The Assessment," as it was commonly referred to, called for the renewal of the leadership organization, claiming the nuns were in doctrinal error and citing three key areas of concern: (1) the "problematic" content of addresses at the LCWR's Annual Assemblies, which the Catholic Church argued not only posed a challenge to "core Catholic beliefs" but was a "rejection of faith" and "serious source of scandal . . . incompatible with religious life"; (2) the policies of corporate dissent surrounding questions of female ordination and homosexuality; and (3) the themes of radical feminism. Furthermore, while acknowledging the nuns' work on issues of social justice,[1] the report criticized their heavy emphasis on these efforts while not promoting the Church's right-to-life mission, particularly noting their silence on abortion. The Assessment was also critical of an affiliate of the LCWR, the Catholic social justice lobby, NETWORK (Vatican Congregation for the Doctrine of the Faith 2012).

Throughout the document outlining the Assessment were calls for obedience and allegiance of religious congregations to the bishops and for greater collaboration between the United States Conference of Catholic Bishops (USCCB) and the LCWR. The two calls cannot be dissociated since the Assessment expressed concern in regard to public statements by the nuns that the CDF argued challenged positions "taken by the Bishops, who are the Church's authentic teachers of faith and morals" (Vatican 2012). As a result, the Assessment declared a period of "renewal" of the organization to be overseen by bishops in the United States. Three members of the USCCB were appointed with this task: Bishop Leonard Blair of Toledo, Ohio, Seattle Archbishop Peter Sartain, and Bishop Thomas Paprocki of Springfield, Illinois (Vatican 2012).

In a statement responding to the rebuke, the LCWR called the claims "unsubstantiated," expressing concern that it could "compromise" the nuns' work in fulfilling "their mission." In a July 2012 interview with National Public Radio, then president of the LCWR, Sister Pat Farrell, noted that the report was more concerned about what the nuns were not speaking out on and was critical of their efforts on issues of social justice (NPR 2012a).

At issue in this dispute is the idea that Catholic women religious are aware that, by institutional design, they do not have formal "authority" to change official doctrine on issues or to change the Church's priorities. This fact cannot be separated from their gender. Therefore, as I explore in this book, some female religious take markedly different approaches in navigating institutional constraints in an effort to live out their religious vocation and impact social policy. These approaches are rooted in their experience as women religious working more directly with the laity than the hierarchy. They derive authority from their professional expertise and from the reforms of Vatican II, which called religious congregations to more authentically live out the mission of their respective orders and adapt to the needs of contemporary society (*Perfectae Caritatis* 1965).

Female religious have long been viewed as caregivers. Due to this experience and the level of expertise noted above, female religious have grown to possess a sense of authority in issues impacting the laity, engaging in social issue–oriented activities. Meanwhile, religious institutions have traditionally viewed men as the decision makers, designing the structure and legalistic rules of the faith (Finlay 1996; Heyer-Gray 2000; Lehman 1994; McDuff 2001; Watling 2002). These factors can cause tension between the male hierarchy and female religious, as both make claims to areas of authority and argue their actions come from authentically living out the faith.

Therefore, the purpose of this book is to examine this very tension of policy and authority within the gendered nature of the Catholic Church and evaluate the level of influence female religious have on various social policy issues. The Assessment of the LCWR, along with an examination of female religious leadership, provides an opportunity to look at how women religious work to fulfill their vocations and make claim to areas of policy expertise, meanwhile navigating institutional constraints of the Catholic Church, some of which are a result of their gender and inability to be members of the clergy. Women have often been viewed as subordinate to male dominance in religion and previous studies have examined this type of gender inequality and tactics women of faith employ to work around institutional barriers, but none have yet to examine this within the context of the Assessment or how policy statements and approaches of female religious may influence the laity (Charlton 1997; Chaves 1997; Dufour 2000; Finlay 1996; Holm and Bowker 1998; Nesbitt 1997; E. Thompson 1991; Watling 2002).

In looking closely at the accusations of the Assessment via a comparison of policy statements between the LCWR and the USCCB, I argue that in most areas of social concern the two groups are not dissimilar in their positions. However, on key issues such as health care, homosexuality, and gender roles, the two organizations differ due to this tension between policy and authority, resulting in the LCWR taking more inclusive positions rooted in their call to social justice.

This came to a crescendo with the LCWR's support of the 2010 Affordable Care Act (ACA), to which the bishops at that time were deeply opposed due to their concerns that the bill would federally fund abortion and require religious employers to cover reproductive care, such as birth control. Both groups spoke of and prioritized health care differently. The sisters' position was rooted in their gendered perspective and the nonclerical role they have working with the laity. For the bishops, their stance was rooted in the institutional positions on procreation and conception. Some women religious and laity suggest it is these disparate positions that really prompted the call for the hierarchy to formally issue the Doctrinal Assessment against the LCWR. However, I argue this does not mean that these women religious were in complete opposition to the Church as the Assessment claims.

I weigh in on this debate by asking two critical questions: (1) Are the sisters and the male clergy in fact in disagreement? and (2) Do women religious have influence? I address these questions through a series of interviews, showing how female religious navigate institutional constraints in the face of scrutiny and within a Church that does not have a consistent culture of promoting female leadership. Furthermore, through a national survey of Catholics, I conduct an experimental analysis, demonstrating that the laity can still be resistant to social policy messages and cues from female religious leadership and authority via a direct examination of statements from the LCWR and USCCB. Last, I provide insight on where the role and influence of women religious is headed in the twenty-first century in the American Catholic Church.

The Assessment: Timeline and Key Groups Involved

In examining the Assessment, it is first important to provide a brief context of the key groups involved, along with a timeline of related events. As mentioned above, the Vatican's CDF officially released the Assessment of the LCWR in April 2012. A doctrinal assessment is issued if an organization within the Catholic

Church is taking positions that are considered counter to official Church teaching. As a result, the organization and its publications, activities, and governing bodies come under review. As stated by Saint John Paul II, "The duty to the Congregation for the Doctrine of the Faith is to promote and safeguard the doctrine on the faith and morals throughout the Catholic world: for this reason everything which in any way touches such matters falls within its competence" (Vatican 1988). The roots of the Assessment stem back over a decade, starting in 2001, when representatives of the LCWR were warned and asked by the CDF to report on their organization's reception of Church teaching regarding the priesthood, homosexuality, and the CDF's 2000 document, *Dominus Iesus*, which summarizes the Catholic faith, emphasizes the ecclesiastical role of the magisterium, and reaffirms the revelation of Jesus Christ as definitive (Levada 2009; Duin 2009; Fox 2009).

The Vatican's Congregation for the Institutes of Consecrated Life and Societies of Apostolic Life began a three-year investigation in 2008, referred to as an "apostolic visitation" of U.S. women religious, and submitted a final report to Rome in 2011. During this time, in early 2009, the then prefect of the CDF, Cardinal William Levada, issued a letter to the LCWR, notifying the sisters that his office had begun the process of assessment of their leadership organization. In the spring of 2009, the LCWR informed its members of the assessment and met with members of the CDF in Rome. At its Annual Assembly in August 2009, the LCWR issued a request for more information as to the cause for the investigation and affirmed its cooperation. The LCWR would continue meetings with the CDF in 2010, along with Bishop Blair, a member of the USCCB (*National Catholic Reporter* 2014).

On April 18, 2012, the Vatican's CDF officially released the document outlining the Doctrinal Assessment of the LCWR, discussing its cause for investigation and process for the organization's renewal. The official document called for a five-year renewal period, along with the coordination of the USCCB and the three delegate bishops appointed to oversee the mandate in working and cooperating with the LCWR in achieving the

Assessment's goals (Vatican Congregation for the Doctrine of the Faith 2012).

On March 13, 2013, Pope Francis was elected pontiff of the Roman Catholic Church; by April, to the disappointment of the LCWR, he reaffirmed the Assessment under the leadership of the new prefect of the CDF, Archbishop Gerhard Muller (McElwee 2013). The Assessment would continue for two additional years, when on April 16, 2015, the CDF accepted a final joint report on the renewal by the LCWR and U.S. delegate bishops, concluding the period of oversight of the organization (Carey 2015).

Although the Assessment has officially concluded, there is still much to be learned about its claims, the gendered-institutional dynamics in which it took place, and what it says about the tension on issues of policy and authority that exist between some female religious and the male-dominated clergy. No study to date has sought to examine the statements of the LCWR to determine if (and how far apart) they were from Church teaching, particularly the USCCB, as mentioned several times in the Assessment (Vatican 2012). Moreover, the influence of Catholic female religious on the laity is under-studied and the context of the Assessment and the leadership issues it relates to provides an opportunity to fill in these gaps. Therefore, it is in this spirit I press on in discussing the key groups noted in the Assessment and part of this examination.

The United States Conference of Catholic Bishops

The influence of the U.S. Catholic bishops stems back to the American Revolutionary War period, as clergy looked to demonstrate that Catholicism was compatible with American democracy. However, the American Conference of Bishops first began to officially formalize in 1919 during World War I as the National Catholic War Council (NCWC), as a response to a number of economic and social issues. In the same year at the request of Pope Benedict XV, the National Catholic War Council reconfigured to better promote Catholic interests in the United States and became known as the National Catholic Welfare Council (Warner 1995). The next major era for the American bishops came during the Second Vatican Council (Vatican II), which consisted of an assembly of Roman Catholic bishops from 1962 to 1965, concluding with a series of reforms to modernize practices in the Church among the clergy, religious, and laity. During the council, the *Decree on the Pastoral Office of Bishops in the Church* was issued, advocating the creation of offices for services of dioceses and regions. In the United States, the bishops interpreted this to mean the establishment of a national conference to assist them in promoting Catholic social policy. In 1966, the bishops reformed the National Catholic Welfare Council, which became the National Conference of Catholic Bishops (NCCB), an organization under canon law, and also simultaneously established the United States Catholic Conference (USCC) for commenting on public policy and civil law. As these coexisting organizations progressed, so did the American bishops' body of social teaching (Warner 1995). Finally, in 2001, the NCCB and USCC combined, becoming the USCCB. The USCCB represents the Roman Catholic hierarchy in the United States. The bishops themselves (some of whom have been promoted to the status of cardinal) constitute the members of the conference and in representing various dioceses of the American Catholic Church are largely secular priests, meaning they do not belong to a religious order but are ordained from a particular diocese and hence representatives of the institutional Church (Catholic Answers 2011; USCCB 2017a).

It is important to note that even though religious priests and nuns may not serve a particular diocese and report directly to their congregations' superiors, they still technically fall under the authority of the bishop in the area in which they reside and work (*Catechism of the Catholic Church* 2010; Vatican 1965a). Moreover, the USCCB is part of the magisterium of the Roman Catholic Church and, as discussed above with regard to the Assessment, the reason why three American delegate bishops from the conference were tasked with overseeing the renewal of the LCWR (Vatican 2012).

The Leadership Conference of Women Religious

The evolution of the LCWR stems back to the 1950s and 1960s when nuns began to get more engaged in how religious, the institutional Church, and the laity would respond to the modern and changing world. The first leadership organization of women religious on a national level in the United States, the Conference of Major Superiors of Women (CMSW), was formed in 1956 and by 1963 moved its headquarters to Washington, DC. During this time, the CMSW began to apply the reforms called for by Vatican II, held annual assemblies among their members, and, in 1968, formed a liaison committee that would serve as a mechanism of communication between the sisters and the American bishops. By the early 1970s the name of the CMSW was changed to the LCWR. However, a conservative splinter group from the original organization, the CMSW remained, expressing concerns that the LCWR "was deviating from authentic church teaching about the essentials of religious life" (LCWR 2017b).

The LCWR has maintained an active presence in the American Catholic Church, representing female religious throughout the country as a membership organization, consisting of fourteen hundred women religious who are leaders of their congregations in the United States. The members of the LCWR are either elected or appointed leaders of their respective religious congregations and come from a variety of orders. It is through these leaders that the LCWR represents 80 percent of the total fifty-seven thousand women religious in the country.[2] Currently, the LCWR represents well over a hundred different congregations of women religious (LCWR 2017c).

The primary purpose of the LCWR is to serve its members and congregations. In doing this it focuses on leadership development by offering mentorship, along with programs and workshops that focus on spiritual leadership. These activities are done with the goal of helping women religious better address issues of social justice in the United States through their work with the laity and other efforts, such as advocacy and education to help shape public policy.[3]

The Catholic Lobby NETWORK and Nuns on the Bus

It was December 1971 when a group of forty-seven Catholic sisters, inspired by the women's movement, arrived in Washington,

DC, to open up a Catholic lobby promoting social justice policy at the federal level. The decision to create the lobby was a response to the bishops encouraging Catholics to not just carry out acts of charity but get involved in systemic change on issues of social justice. The nuns also saw forming the lobby as a way to live out the reforms of Vatican II, which called for the creation of a more just world. These nuns decided the best way to form their political lobby was to network among already existing social justice organizations and together build relationships with lawmakers on Capitol Hill to affect federal policy. Over the years, the makeup of NETWORK has grown more diverse to include the laity as well as people of all faiths or no faith at all.[4]

As noted in the Assessment, NETWORK as an affiliate of the LCWR came under scrutiny by both the Vatican and the U.S. bishops. Part of this was a result of the 2010 health care debate. In a show of support for the bill on behalf of Catholic female religious, who have a history of building hospitals in the United States and working with vulnerable populations to access affordable care, Sister Simone Campbell, executive director of NETWORK, wrote a letter to Congress endorsing the ACA. The letter was signed by over fifty sisters in leadership positions, including the LCWR (NETWORK 2017; Catholic Medical Association 2010). Again, the USCCB had a long-standing position against the ACA due to its belief that it federally funded abortion and its dislike of the Department of Health and Human Services' mandate for insurers to cover contraception, both of which are against Church teaching. The women religious who signed the letter felt the bill had protections against these issues, particularly for religious employers. Moreover, due to their experience in working with lay women and children, the nuns felt that the bill addressed important elements of reproductive care.[5] This showing of support by NETWORK and the LCWR created more tension between their organizations and the bishops. This tension was evident in a press release the USCCB issued regarding the Assessment, which noted criticism of the LCWR's long-standing relationship with NETWORK (NETWORK 2017; USCCB 2012b).

As noted above, the story of the Assessment became national news and Catholics around the country began showing their support for the nuns, holding rallies and prayer vigils (O'Malley 2012). Seeing this as an opportunity to showcase the social justice work of women religious as well as their lobby, NETWORK decided to launch a "Nuns on the Bus" tour in the summer of 2012. By traveling throughout the country, NETWORK was able to bring attention to its causes and work to consolidate support among the laity regarding the Assessment (NETWORK 2017).

It is important to note that NETWORK, though mentioned in the Assessment, came under criticism but not formal rebuke and review by the hierarchy, unlike the case of the LCWR. Therefore, in this book I examine the LCWR's policy statements and actions but at times discuss the work of NETWORK and other dynamics of the American Catholic Church that are related to issues and challenges of female religious leadership.

Lingering Tension: Religious vs. Clerical Interpretation of Vatican II

Before addressing some of the scholarship that this work relates to and builds on, along with how the analysis of the book proceeds, it is imperative to address some context and lingering issues of Vatican II, because it lays the foundation for the tension between the nuns and the hierarchy that the Assessment captures. In 1959, Pope John XXIII called for an aggiornamento (update) of the Church to bring the faith into modern times. As Western Europe was becoming more secular, the pope saw a need to reform some of the practices of religious life and also call for an increased role among the laity in the life of the Church. The Second Vatican Council commenced in 1962 and would bring forth a series of meetings among the Church's bishops, lasting until its completion in 1965 (Seaman 2013). Notably, women religious were not part of the decision-making process of the council. However, fifteen women in faith leadership positions (seven lay and eight religious) were permitted to attend Vatican II as official observers. The only American nun to attend was Sister Mary Luke Tobin, then president of what would become known as the LCWR (LCWR 2017b). In a 1987 interview with *U.S. Catholic Faith in*

Real Life, Sister Tobin noted that there was excitement around the gathering of Vatican II and her congregation was eager for her to attend the meetings, encouraging her to find out what it meant for religious communities and particularly women.

For these sisters, the answer to these questions would come in the council's release of the 1965 document, *Perfectae Caritatis* (The Adaptation and Renewal of Religious Life). Issued by Pope Paul VI,[6] this document is essential to understanding the tension between policy and authority among the nuns and the hierarchy, because both groups interpreted the reforms of Vatican II somewhat differently. For example, women religious, such as those associated with the now LCWR and affiliates like NETWORK, saw the decree as empowering, affirming the freedom of religious life as opposed to the clerical life of the institutional Church. The document called on the religious to take key steps in modernizing their congregations according to their unique histories and characteristics. It also reaffirmed the leadership of their organizations, noting that the religious were first subordinate to their congregations' superiors. The document also emphasized that the religious' primary responsibility was to live out the Gospel by more directly engaging the laity and working among them. These action steps would be interpreted by the nuns as an opportunity to not only reexamine the missions of their respective congregations but also increase their level of professionalization and education, which the document directly called for. Nuns were supported by their congregations and the Church to become as educated as possible; this ensured that they receive college educations and qualify for various professional careers. Thus, Vatican II brought forth religious women who saw their work not just in terms of a religious calling and duty but in terms of any profession they embarked on being part of their religious vocation if it were used to improve the conditions of people (Ebaugh 1993). This professionalization of American Catholic sisters arguably allowed them to use their professional skills in their social justice work and equipped the nuns with a policy expertise and ability to work in high levels of administration (M. Thompson 1986). As Ebaugh (1993, 404) argues, "Catholics and non-Catholics alike not only accepted the fact that nuns were career women but came to expect excellent service from them . . . In many instances, nuns paved the way for women into new professional areas. This is the case, for example, with hospital administrators, accrediting boards for various institutions, university professors, scientific researchers, university presidents and administrators of social work agencies." Occasionally, this dynamic would put women religious in opposition with the institutional Church, subjecting them to scrutiny, because the hierarchy saw the reforms of Vatican II differently.

This difference in interpretation of the Vatican II reforms can also be seen in the council's 1965 statement, the *Decree on the Pastoral Authority of the Bishops*, and the 2012 document outlining the Doctrinal Assessment of the LCWR. This 1965 decree affirmed that the bishops were not only members of the hierarchy but part of the teaching and governing authority of the Church. The document tasks the bishops with the authority to ensure that evangelization activities be supported by Church teachings and that the religious, though part of different congregations, still be subject to the ordinary authority of local bishops and it emphasized their need to consult with the hierarchy.

Furthermore, in referencing Vatican II, the CDF's Doctrinal Assessment of the LCWR, noted that the indictment against the nuns came during the fiftieth anniversary of the council. In the Assessment, the CDF did not recognize the freedom of religious life, as interpreted by the nuns' understanding of Vatican II, but instead called for their yielding to Church authority stating, "The Second Vatican Council clearly indicates that an authentic teaching of the Church calls for the religious submission of intellect and will" (Vatican 2012). Overall, the Assessment was making it clear that the nuns' focus on social justice, along with some of their publications and speeches "that disagree with or challenge positions taken by the Bishops," was taking the reforms of Vatican II too far in the eyes of the institutional Church (Vatican 2012).

Discussion and Overview of Chapters

In proceeding with an examination of the Assessment and the tension between policy and authority that can exist between male and female religious leadership groups within the Catholic Church, Chapter 2 provides a firsthand look at how nuns navigate the institutional Church to impact social policy. Through a series of interviews with male clergy and female religious (including representatives from the LCWR and NETWORK), this chapter shows the various ways nuns utilize their position outside of the official hierarchy to influence policy and demonstrates the institutional scrutiny they face at times when doing so (e.g., the Doctrinal Assessment of the LCWR). This chapter also highlights some of the differences between religious life and clerical life, which adds to the gender dynamics and tension experienced between the nuns and the hierarchy. The analysis also demonstrates how the gendered nature of the Catholic Church can at times create an environment of lay resistance to female leadership.

Where Chapters 1 and 2 lay the foundation for the tension that can exist between female religious and the male-dominated hierarchy, Chapter 3 begins a direct examination of the Doctrinal Assessment's claims by analyzing the policy statements of the LCWR and the USCCB to evaluate whether the nuns were in fact taking positions counter to Church teaching and calling their audiences to mobilize on these issues. This is important to examine as some researchers find that statements by religious elites can increase engagement and spur political mobilization (Campbell 2004). Clergy use their religious organizations and platforms to inform, bring together, and activate their flocks on a variety of social and political issues (Djupe and Calfano 2014; Olson, Guth, and Guth 2003; Wilcox and Jelen 2003; Wilcox and Sigelman 2001). Wilcox and Sigelman (2001) specifically examine how religious institutions encourage their congregants to vote via placing voting guides in their churches. Moreover, the USCCB clearly states in their key civic engagement publication, *Forming Consciences for Faithful Citizenship* (2007), that "during election years, there may be many handouts and voter guides that are produced and distributed. We encourage Catholics to seek those resources authorized by their own bishops, their state Catholic conference, and the United States Conference of Catholic Bishops" (10).

Focusing more on Catholic women religious, Brigham (2015) argues that mobilized activities such as the LCWR's traveling *Women and Spirit* exhibit, highlighting the work of American Catholic nuns was a way for the sisters to mobilize and engage the public, gaining support for the social service work they do. And as previously noted, the Catholic sisters participating in Nuns on the Bus used the tours to mobilize the public on a variety issues, such as immigration reform and health care. These tours also encourage people to vote on and advocate for an end to unlimited campaign spending (or what is referred to as "dark money") by political action committees via the Supreme Court's 2010 decision in *Citizens United v. FEC*. This particular tour, launched in the fall of 2014 consisted of holding seventy-five events in over thirty-six cities across the country, prompting even the attention and attendance of then vice president Joe Biden (Jenkins 2014).

These examples demonstrate that both male and female religious have mobilized on political and social issues and, at times, have called the laity to participate in their efforts. Therefore, in analyzing leadership groups within the American Catholic Church, it is important to assess whether their statements call their congregations to mobilize and, if so, on what issues. It is also important to examine if they call their audiences to certain types of activities. This helps answer a couple of significant questions: (1) Does the LCWR mobilize on issues counter to those of the USCCB (and hence the Church)? (2) Are there differences between these two groups in terms of how they mobilize and/or what issues they prioritize in their mobilization efforts? Overall, this examination adds to the literature on how religious institutions mobilize their flock on political issues and sheds light on any gendered differences in these efforts.

Continuing with the content analysis of the LCWR and USCCB's policy statements, Chapter 4 turns its attention to the language style and frames used by these groups in their messages. This chapter continues examining the claims of the Doctrinal Assessment to identify if these factors add to the belief that the nuns' stances were in conflict with the bishops and hence the Church. This chapter poses the question, Do the language styles and frames (e.g., points of emphasis) in these organizations' policy statements differ and, if so, how? For example, does the USCCB employ a more orthodox and masculine language style and the LCWR a more feminine and progressive language style? Do either or both of these organizations emphasize frames in their statements to bolster their positions, such as Catholic social teaching, natural law, or conscience protection? What does this tell us about the claims of the Doctrinal Assessment, as well as differences between these two leadership groups?

Through a national survey experiment of over one thousand Catholics, Chapter 5 poses the question, Do the LCWR's and the USCCB's policy statements influence lay public opinion? It is important to examine if Catholic religious elites have the potential to influence the laity on policy issues, as Catholics comprise about 20 percent of the electorate and are the largest single-faith group in the United States (Gray 2015). Scholars argue that religious leaders are in the position and have the capacity to influence public opinion (Campbell 2004; Djupe and Calfano 2014; Djupe and Gilbert 2002; Jones-Correa and Leal 2001; Olson, Crawford, and Deckman 2005; Wald 1992). However, compared to Protestant religious elites, analyses on Catholic clergy's influence on the laity via their policy statements is still very much developing. This effort is even more scant with regard to Catholic female religious. Regarding Catholic clergy, Wald (1992) found that there was an increased (though short-lived) level of support among Catholics for a decrease of defense spending with the issuance of the American bishops 1983 statement, *The Challenge of Peace Pastoral: God's Promise and Our Response.* In examining the influence of Pope John Paul II, Mulligan (2006) found that Catholics who found the pontiff favorable were more likely to share the Church's position against the death penalty and abortion. Furthermore, on the issue of capital punishment, Bjarnason and Welch (2004) found that Catholic priests yield significant influence, especially among parishioners who are more spiritual and less politically and socially conservative. Calfano and Oldmixon (2016) discuss how the bishops' influence over Catholics is inconsistent and limited with regard to priests' political behavior. In looking at material distributed to parishioners in Florida dioceses during the 2012 election, Holman and Shockley (2017) found as information is filtered down from the USCCB to state conferences of bishops and to local parishes, the political messages received by the laity from priests varies. The authors argue this complicates providing a congruent message on the Church's teaching and positions on political issues. However, this study and others have not accounted for the bishops' (nor the nuns') level of influence when Catholics are immediately exposed to their messages and/or statement source cues.

Chapter 5 helps fill in these gaps in evaluating if Catholic religious leadership groups, such as the USCCB and LCWR, have the ability to influence Catholic public opinion via direct and immediate exposure to their statements. Furthermore, this chapter connects back to the theme and discussion on the tension of policy and authority between the nuns and the hierarchy, as it examines if lay Catholics are more willing to be influenced on social issues by either a male or a female leadership group within the Church. Being a gendered institution that places a premium on male clerical leadership, are Catholics more prone to be influenced by policy messages and cues by the bishops or the nuns? Who do laity see as an immediate authority upon exposure to their social policy statements? Moreover, as the Catholic Church is an institution rooted in a culture of authority, hierarchy, and patriarchy, are lay Catholics with a predisposition to authority more likely to be influenced by the USCCB or LCWR, particularly on key issues addressed in the Assessment, like homosexuality and female ordination? Chapters 3 and 4 provide a sense of whether or not the hierarchy had valid concerns for issuing the Assessment through an examination of the nuns' and bishops' policy statements, but Chapter 5 provides insight into whether the hierarchy needed to be concerned that the LCWR had the potential to influence lay Catholics in the direction of their positions. Overall, was the LCWR a threat to the gendered dynamics and authority of the hierarchy?

Finally, Chapter 6 discusses the key takeaways and findings from this analysis, showing what can be learned from the claims of the Doctrinal Assessment and about female leadership in the American Catholic Church. Dealing with the realities of a clergy and nun shortage, along with a decreasing number of practicing Catholics, what impact if any do the USCCB and female religious leaders, like those affiliated with the LCWR, have on the laity and the Church in general? In looking at Pope Francis's new Commission on the Female Diaconate, will female religious' position of authority in the Church be elevated or will they need to continue to navigate institutional constraints indefinitely? Essentially this final chapter brings together a discussion on what was learned from this examination of male clergy and female religious in the American Catholic Church, along with what challenges still exists and where the faith is currently headed in terms of leadership models and roles.

2

Navigating the Hierarchy

A Look at Female and Male Religious Leadership, Political Engagement, and Influences

The hierarchy of the Catholic Church consists of ordained clergy, beginning with the pope, head of the institutional Church and Vatican. Following the head of the Church are other administrative members such as cardinals, who are appointed by the pontiff and whose main responsibilities consist of advising the holy father and running their various assigned posts. Next, the hierarchy consists of archbishops, who oversee a main or metropolitan diocese, followed by bishops, who administer a particular diocese and provide pastoral governance to their assigned stations. Priests who work in a diocese fall under the administration of their local bishop and, as ordained ministers, are responsible for administering mass and most sacraments. Priests can belong to a religious order (e.g., Franciscans) or a diocese (e.g., Chicago). Finally, deacons are ordained ministers who assist in performing sacraments, except for the Eucharist, anointing of the sick, and confession. It is apparent that female religious (and the laity) are left out of the formal clerical leadership model and that the institutional Church is a gendered system, implying that the dynamics between males and females can enact situations of dominance and subordination, as well as the creation of alliances and exclusions (Acker 1990; Katzenstein 1995; 1998;

Stalp and Winders 2002). This institutional dynamic highlights the gendered nature of authority in the Church and the traditional view of religion in general, where men are seen as the symbol of leadership, the guardians of doctrine, and women are seen as inferior and therefore unsuitable for certain roles and posts within the faith (Charlton 2000; King 1989; Lummis and Nesbitt 2000; McGuire 1997; Nesbitt 1997; O'Connor 1995; Sered 1997). In this environment, how do women religious navigate or maneuver around these institutional constraints in order to take action on social policy issues and effect change? Some argue that one key to this maneuvering lies in a lack of ties to the official hierarchy. Female religious have learned to utilize their existence outside of the institutional Church to exercise varying degrees of mobility, influence, freedom, and autonomy in order to influence social policy (Ebaugh 1993; Katzenstein 1998; Stalp and Winders 2002). At times, this maneuvering has placed women religious in an oppositional stance with the hierarchy. However, using their position outside of the institution has enabled them to carry out their mission and commitment to Catholic social teaching in a personal way, something that some argue directly engages with the people and fosters public support and personal authority (Brigham 2015; Carroll 1981).

I agree with the previous scholarship noted above that, yes, Catholic women religious are able to utilize their position outside of the institutional Church to effect social change. However, part of their strategy is also knowing when it works to the advantage of their social policy objectives to collaborate with the hierarchy. Assessing the shape and extent of this collaboration brings new perspective to how religious gendered organizations are navigated by women religious. Scholars such as Stalp and Winders (2002) find that when priests participate in activism, they can incur more negative consequences due to their position within the institution than women religious. I argue that when Catholic sisters and nuns act out independently of the official Church on a policy issue, they tend to do so in the name of their own religious congregations or as individual sisters, exacting their own authority as women religious. Yet this approach may still not safeguard them from institutional scrutiny, but instead it provides women religious a different space and way of speaking out in opposition, which is markedly different from the clergy or even a Catholic sister working for a local diocese overseen by a bishop.

To examine these issues, I conducted interviews with Catholic female religious, several members of the clergy, and two lay individuals. In total, fourteen subjects are included in this study, five ordained members of the clergy, six current and one former Catholic women religious (who served in organizations such as the LCWR, NETWORK, diocesan leadership positions, and in various capacities through their respective religious congregations), and two lay Catholics (one female and one male chosen for their unique work with women religious and clergy). These discussions provide rich insight into how female religious are able to navigate around formal barriers of the hierarchy to impact social policy, and how collaborating at times with the official Church (i.e., the USCCB) can also work to advance their policy goals. These discussions also show the various challenges that occur when women are tied to the institutional Church.

Catholic Women Religious and the Institutional Church

In her work on how women religious bring a different type of public face to Catholicism in the United States, Erin Brigham (2015) discusses how the LCWR, through its traveling national museum exhibit *Women in Spirit* and NETWORK's Nuns on the Bus tour, provides venues at which sisters use their experiences to challenge the bishops' authority and engage in the public realm. These events helped the sisters bring attention to important issues and showcase their policy expertise and sense of authority on certain social topics, like immigration reform and advocating for a federal budget better situated to combat poverty. Through their efforts, nuns show a new way of being Church, focused on the needs of the marginalized, collegial leadership, and dialogue with the laity.

Some sisters represent a different type of Church through an alternative public discourse that embraces Catholic social teaching, feminist theology, and the reforms of Vatican II (Brigham 2015). Again, Vatican II (1962–1965) was considered the most significant and consequential event in the life of the Church during the twentieth century by encouraging the religious and laity to take a more participatory role in the life of the Church and, as some argue, fostered a deeper sense of independence among Catholic nuns (Burns 1992; Flannery 1998; Wallace 1988).

Stalp and Winders (2002) argue that congregations of women religious represent a more democratic model of leadership. In arguing against a strictly male, noninclusive hierarchy, Schüssler Fiorenza (2002) advocates that the Church should be better equated with the egalitarian ideals of the early Christian communities, which is not the essence of the male-dominated hierarchy of the Catholic Church in which there is a clear divide between the ordained clergy and the nonordained and where women religious are seen as complimentary and subordinate to the male-dominated clergy. Despite this institutional dynamic, some Catholic women religious have taken their vocations of social justice to the political sphere, seeing their efforts intertwined in what Olson, Crawford, and Deckman (2005) refer to as a "religiopolitical calling."

It is important to note that work on female religious is a developing field. Most work on female religious' ability to influence social policy and public opinion and/or be politically engaged focuses on those that are clergy in Protestant denominations (Adams 2007; Djupe and Olson 2013; Olson, Guth, and Guth 2003; Olson, Crawford, and Deckman 2005). Some works discuss female religious positions outside of the hierarchy and how these roles can be tied to a level of freedom and mobility not experienced by diocesan priests (Ebaugh 1993; Katzenstein 1995, 1998; Stalp and Winders 2002). However, these works do not make a direct connection to how this institutional positioning may help make a public policy impact and influence the laity or enhance their own level of social engagement as religious.

Therefore, this chapter accomplishes three things. First, it is able to directly discuss examples of how female religious working outside the hierarchy's supervision have the potential to affect already existing social policy. Next, it provides examples of when it is beneficial for female religious to join efforts with the institutional Church, demonstrating that knowledge of when to integrate with it is part of this maneuvering to impact policy. Last, it discusses how women religious can find themselves in tension with the institutional Church via a discussion of the Doctrinal Assessment of the LCWR. This chapter concludes with a discussion of some of the current implications for the future of female religious life.

Interview Selection Process and Methodology

Subjects to interview were selected on the basis of either their membership in the clergy or their position in working closely with clergy and women religious. Furthermore, since this work also examines the scrutiny of the LCWR (and their affiliate NETWORK) brought on by the Doctrinal Assessment, representatives from these organizations were contacted. Interview subjects also included a representative from the group Conference of Major Superiors of Women Religious (CMSWR), who were once affiliated with the LCWR. Next, diocesan priests were considered and included into the study. During the interviews, interviewees referred others who were subsequently contacted. For example, this approach led to the analysis encompassing interviews with female pastoral coordinators, which some bishops have appointed to run parishes in light of the priest shortage. This position was first formally articulated in the Church's 1983 Code of Canon Law (517, §2), stating that the position of pastoral coordinator is a person "endowed with the powers and faculties of a pastor to supervise the pastoral care" of the parish. The pastoral coordinator is a professional minister responsible for officially administering the parish and is supervised by a priest moderator or supervisor (CARA 2005). Including female subjects who hold this position and are therefore tied to the diocese becomes essential in assessing women religious' ability to politically engage within and outside of the institutional Church.

A total of fourteen interviews were conducted from the spring of 2016 through early winter of 2017. The interview pool consisted of one retired priest; one priest-pastor; a reverend; a monsignor; Bishop Cantu of the Diocese of Las Cruces, New Mexico (also a member of the USCCB); one sister from the LCWR; Sister Simone Campbell, the executive director of NETWORK; one sister who served as a pastoral coordinator for several dioceses across the country; one former Catholic sister; three sisters currently belonging to religious orders (one was active in Future Church, one was affiliated with the LCWR while serving in leadership for her congregation, and one was a member of the CMSWR).[1] Last, one lay woman serving as a pastoral coordinator and one lay male who works with the Conference of Major Superiors of Men (CMSM) were interviewed.[2]

Working Within and Outside of the Institutional Church

Political Engagement

It is no surprise that these religious elites have been politically involved—almost all clergy are involved at least at a moderate level (Djupe and Gilbert 2002; Guth et al. 1997). All fourteen subjects discussed they had been politically and civically engaged, meaning at some point they took part in the political process by taking action on issues of public concern.[3] For example, the priest and pastor interviewed discussed how they had been part of persuading parishioners to sign petitions on issues ranging from immigration reform and opposing the ACA and the contraception mandate to trying to stop California's right-to-die legislation for terminally ill patients. The pastor expressed how he felt that these efforts had the potential to influence Catholic public opinion. He also went on to reference the USCCB's 2007 document, *Forming Conscience for Faithful Citizenship*, discussing how the bishops, via official communication, reminded the dioceses of this literature on a Catholic's responsibility to be politically and civically engaged during the 2016 election season. The pastor was careful to say, however, that he could not endorse a candidate due to the Church's 501(c)(3) tax-exempt status. He also commented that any political engagement activity in which he is involved takes place at the direction and permission of his bishop, stating "I take my vow of obedience to the bishop seriously."

In discussing this issue with the monsignor, he shared that he had been very politically engaged on local issues facing his community, such as homelessness and mental health. He discussed how he worked with local policy makers, community stakeholders, and even his congressman to draw attention to these matters. However, he did share some frustration with how the bishops handle politically oriented information. He stated, "We're told we cannot say anything during an election, but are given information on an issue, then they tie our hands by telling us you can't preach about that." He further discussed that then when clergy do get information on a social policy issue from the bishop, it can come within just a few short days of Sunday mass and so there is limited time to educate themselves or their congregation on the topic.

Bishop Cantu of the Diocese of La Cruces in New Mexico discussed how he worked with priests in the diocese to disseminate informational and educational "Action Alerts" on public policy topics so that local diocesan priests could share the bishops' positions with parishioners. Bishop Cantu explained that these alerts are meant to mobilize the laity to take action on a policy issue, such as contacting their legislator and advocating the Church's position.

While we were discussing these issues with these male members of the clergy, I asked them about the ability of women religious to be politically engaged. All agreed that women religious had more freedom as figures outside of the institutional Church. For instance, the pastor stated, "Being non-ordained allows women religious more freedom of movement and at times greater freedom in terms of what they say. They are not tied to a parish and not tied sacramentally the same way priests are."

The women religious interviewed also hit on the same theme. Due to their positions outside of the hierarchy, it became apparent that they felt more "free" to be active on political issues. On the other hand, one sister in the sample was hesitant to discuss her engagement as "political" and showed more deference to the institutional Church. To give insight into her positions, it may be worth noting that this sister is part of a conservative leadership organization, the CMSWR, which split from the more progressive leadership group, the LCWR. This particular sister stressed that CMSWR was not a political group and supported the teachings of the Catholic Church, particularly on respecting life. This was captured in her community's support for the Church in *Zubik v. Burwell* (2016), a case in which Little Sisters of the Poor, the international congregation who provides care to the elderly, argued that the contraception mandate in the ACA violated their religious beliefs.[4] This sister spoke about how members of her community marched in Washington, DC, and also wrote an amicus curiae brief to the Court advocating that sisters not be required to accommodate the mandate.

Other sister participants discussed their political engagement outside the institutional Church. For example, a sister with the LCWR discussed how not being ordained allows women religious to work with the most marginalized groups of society in an intimate way because, "we are closer to folks, we're present with folks in the streets. That's our vocation. Ordained clergy have a similar mission, but perhaps because of other obligations, don't have the same kind of opportunities that we have to be really present." She further elaborated that due to sisters' involvement in social service work women religious are able to influence public policy and the laity.

However, this particular sister did also share that the LCWR at times does work in collaboration with USCCB. In her role as a social justice promoter she attends meetings at the USCCB as a member of the conference's staff justice working groups. In this capacity she is not necessarily taking direction from the bishops but providing information and working with other organizations to shape policy, by going back to her fellow members and advocating positions on issues, as well as lobbying Congress. For example, she discussed how she sits on the bishops' Justice for Immigrants working group, where she assists with policy development for immigration reform. This showcases how some women religious are able to work within and outside the institutional Church in terms of political engagement.

Not being clergy appears to create a zone in which some sisters have more mobility and autonomy to advocate for certain policies, while simultaneously utilizing opportunities to collaborate with the institutional Church. Therefore, this too may be part of the navigational process, knowing when political engagement is best done outside the institution and when it calls for collaboration with it. For example, one of the subjects who works closely with the male counterpart organization of the LCWR, the CMSM, and is on USCCB staff working committees, discussed how members of Congress and their staff see the voice of the Catholic Church on Capitol Hill as what the bishops' positions are on issues. Despite there being eight to ten different Catholic organizations in Washington, DC, he explained, due to the size, the position in the hierarchy, and the amount of resources, the USCCB is viewed as the authoritative and definitive source. This sentiment parallels Walter Mondale's 1984 campaign manager Robert Beckel's sentiment, "If you are a bishop, you've got a lot of people, you've got money, places to meet, you've got a lot [of] things that any good politician would like to have at his disposal" (Ross Sammon 2008, 17).

Sister Simone Campbell, executive director of the Catholic lobby NETWORK also shared how not being institutionally tied allows her and her organization to more fully carry out their work of social justice. When asked if not being clergy allowed female religious to be more engaged in public policy, Sister Simone stated, "I think it absolutely does. I mean experience says that it does. Because this is the thing that annoys our hierarchy. And that we're not controllable and in a top down authoritarian model." Sister Simone further elaborated that, because she is not ordained, she does not have to preside at a parish every weekend, giving her the freedom to be politically engaged. The Nuns on the Bus tour serves as an example of this. She went on to discuss this dynamic as one of the differences between religious life and the life of secular priests (those belonging to a diocese). She explained how the religious report to a superior in their congregations, so one is free to carry out one's mission. These points made by Sister Simone Campbell demonstrate that women religious can experience two related forms of freedom compared to their male clerical counterparts: (1) since they are religious and therefore not tied to a diocese, they are not directly accountable to the institutional hierarchy; and (2) because they are not tied to a diocese they are inevitably less accountable to Catholics in the pews since they are not carrying out Church services, such as the administration of the Eucharist, confessions, baptism, and so on. She expressed how Pope Francis understands the importance of religious life and why it's different from diocesan and clerical life, pointing out that "he is a Jesuit, and he knows the freedom of religious life, and so some of the way he is being Pope is out of the freedom of religious life, which is very different than the male leadership brought up in diocesan seminaries, getting promoted, doing the rules. It's a very different reality." Other interviewees agreed. The lay male Catholic from the CMSM discussed how Pope Francis is trying to model a more pastoral, less administrative approach to the American bishops, to which he felt some are resistant.

Institutional Scrutiny

Scrutiny toward female religious in the Catholic Church is not new. Some have discussed the scrutiny that sisters have received in more contemporary times as rooted in the interpretation and application of the reforms called for by Vatican II. Sisters found a new sense of independence with some leaving the convent and moving closer to the neighborhoods they served. Some sisters shed their habits, which during the medieval period were worn by orders such as the Benedictines and Dominicans as a way of distinguishing themselves as consecrated to God. However, the habit was also considered the "working costume" of the time and other orders wore it to blend in to the communities they served (Kuhns 2005). This latter point was emphasized by several sisters, who shared that, since the habit originated and was contemporary centuries ago, they too now needed to wear the dress of the day—simple, plain, contemporary clothing—which is easier for them to work in. Some shared they felt less pious and more approachable out of a habit. As Sister Helen Prejean shared in an

NPR interview, "We dressed in these black habits from head to toe. We scared a lot of kids" (Bradley Hagerty 2012, para. 6). An antiquated debate for some, this shift in clothing caused tension with the Church, particularly with those who had a more conservative interpretation of the reforms of Vatican II.

Furthermore, as Bradley Hagerty (2012) discusses, one of the first public conflicts between the sisters and the Church came during Pope John Paul II's 1979 visit to the United States, during which religious leader Sister Theresa Kane addressed the pope by asking the Church to include women in all ministries of the institution. During this address, several dozen nuns stood, adorning blue armbands as a sign of support for female ordination. Julia Lieblich's (1992), *Sisters Lives of Devotion and Defiance* discusses other sisters who have also placed themselves in opposition to the Church due to their political positions. For example, she discusses how in 1984, Sister Donna Quinn fell under the Vatican's rebuke for being one of ninety-seven signers to a *New York Times* ad calling for a dialogue on abortion and addressing the diversity of public opinion on the subject among Catholics. Quinn's "marginal" status outside of the institutional Church did not fully protect her from Church scrutiny and rebuke, as the Vatican called for her and the others to publicly retract their positions on the issue, threatening them with dismissals from their religious congregations if they did not comply. In the end, Sister Quinn did not personally stand down to the Vatican; however, her congregation sent a letter to Rome clarifying her position as not promoting abortion. Sister Quinn was later cleared by the Vatican but expressed that if she had to do it all over again, she would insist on communicating directly with Rome so that she could state her position on her own terms.

In discussing the Assessment with the sisters interviewed here, some shared the reason they felt the LCWR came under scrutiny. Some believed it occurred as a result of the LCWR and NETWORK's public support of the ACA in 2010. The bishops were opposed to the ACA primarily due to the contraception mandate and their belief the bill federally funded abortion.[5] One sister discussed how her congregation signed the letter written by Sister

Simone Campbell supporting the ACA. As mentioned in the previous chapter, this letter was sent to Congress and signed by over fifty leaders of Catholic Sisters Communities, including the LCWR, urging legislators "to cast a life-affirming yes vote" to the bill, expressing that as religious sisters in this country,

> we have witnessed firsthand the impact of our national health care crisis, particularly its impact on women, children and people who are poor. We see the toll on families who have delayed seeking care due to lack of health insurance coverage or lack of funds with which to pay high deductibles . . . while it is an imperfect measure, it is a crucial next step in realizing health care for all . . . and despite false claims to the contrary, the Senate bill will not provide taxpayer funding for elective abortions. It will uphold longstanding conscience protections and it will make historic new investments—$250 million in support of pregnant women. This is the REAL pro-life stance, and we as Catholics are all for it.[6]

The letter was not published in the name of the Church but instead as women religious, an example of how nuns exercise their personal sense of authority, rooted in their policy expertise on issues such as health care and the sense of accountability they feel to the laity. This demonstrates the navigation and maneuvering around the institutional constraints of the Church that sisters find themselves doing in order to take a policy position. However, it does not always safeguard them, as witnessed by the Doctrinal Assessment.

The impetus for the Assessment may also reflect an intense prioritization on abortion by the bishops. As noted, the Assessment criticized the LCWR for its silence on the issue. Some sisters argued that abortion is not the only pro-life issue; the social justice issues they are engaged in are also. As one sister stated, "A lot of the bishops in the U.S., they only have one note and that is getting better, but I would say, it's the abortion issue and they call themselves pro-life, but they ignore immigration, poverty, education, all sorts of things that from my perspective are pro-life issues." Some sisters also spoke of the fact that when they are serving people through their respective ministries, it is not their place to judge but only to help the people form their own conscience.

The scrutiny that the LCWR and NETWORK received may have appeared to have a negative impact; however, in talking with individuals currently or once affiliated with these groups, such as Sister Simone Campbell, they agreed it was overwhelmingly positive in terms of the support received from both Catholics and non-Catholics. As a result of this support they gained donations that provided needed resources to poorer religious congregations. As some explained, religious congregations are expected to be financially self-sustaining; therefore, the ability to help those who are struggling was beneficial. One sister stated, "It really led to a lot of free publicity on what women religious were doing and their contributions." As Sister Simone Campbell shared, "It was for what the spirit did. So, from my perspective the Holy Spirit took the conflict, lifted it up and we as women religious know how much support we have in the United States and we would have never known it otherwise . . . we would have never had Nuns on the Bus," whose impact she feels "finally lifted up poverty in our nation—and we contributed to it being talked about as a nation."

The Doctrinal Assessment came to an unexpected conclusion April 16, 2015, at a meeting at the Vatican. The CDF accepted a final report on the Assessment, marking its completion. Both the Vatican and LCWR noted that the renewal concluded with a spirit of "cooperation." In an official statement, the LCWR went on to thank Pope Francis for his leadership during the time of the renewal, which concluded two years into his papacy (McElwee 2015).

In discussing the conclusion of the Assessment with the subjects interviewed, the monsignor and several sisters expressed a sense of relief it had ended positively. The monsignor shared that he felt Pope Francis's fairly quick conclusion of the Assessment was a way of standing up for the sisters. He felt Pope Benedict XVI had attacked the nuns, stating, "Their (meaning the sisters involved) spirits was just devastated—they are thinking we have been out there working and now you attack us? Pope Francis very much validated their work." Some also shared that the institutional scrutiny did not work out in the Church's favor. One sister said it was "an embarrassment for the institutional Church, because so many, particularly here in this country rose to the defense of women religious." Sister Simone Campbell stated that the Church did not necessarily get what it wanted, "but what they got surprised them. It was a process that was unusual, because it came from a contemplative stance. The Catholic Sisters did not do the usual oppositional politic, they came in dialogue and prayer. I think that it had an impact on the bishops." In the aftermath of the Assessment's conclusion, the LCWR released a statement on its website stating the "sanctions called for in the CDF mandate were disproportionate to the concerns raised" and that "they were deeply saddened that the report caused scandal and pain throughout the Catholic community." The organization also remained consistent in its view that the accusations against the LCWR were false (LCWR 2015).

Women Leadership in the Institutional Church: A Look at Female Pastoral Coordinators

It is important to include a discussion of those who work inside the Church, particularly in a diocesan capacity where they are at the direction of the bishop. This helps assess whether these are gendered dynamics or institutional ones. It is also important to consider women religious' activities within the institutional hierarchy as more than half of parish staff comprises women (49 percent lay and 3 percent religious sisters). Moreover, lay ecclesial ministers (LEM), defined as "paid, non-ordained parish ministry staff working at least 20 hours a week" (Gray, Gautier, and Cidade 2011) have increased, comprising 21,569 (including vowed religious) in the early 1990s to a currently projected amount of over 37,000. LEMs can be women religious, such as those who serve in the capacity as pastoral coordinator for a diocesan parish (Gray, Gautier, and Cidade 2011). Pastoral coordinators are professional ministers sent at the request of the diocesan bishop to officially administer the duties and responsibilities of a parish. One of the reasons this position was instituted was to more effectively handle the priest shortage in parishes. In 1965, the Center for Applied Research in the Apostolate (CARA) at Georgetown University reported that there were a total of 35,925 diocesan priests, which dropped down to 25,868 in 2015 (CARA 2017). As reported by Leah Libresco (2015), 20 percent of parishes in the United States currently have no priest in residence, which has led to responsibilities in administration of the parish falling under pastoral coordinators in some cases.

Two female subjects in this study provided information from the perspective of a pastoral coordinator, one a religious sister and the other lay. Both have served as a pastoral coordinator for multiple parishes, one for a total of sixteen years and the other for several decades. In sharing how they came to be pastoral coordinators, they expressed a call and sense of duty to serve the Church in a leadership role.

In discussing their experiences as female pastoral coordinators, it became evident that the position comes with its own constraints and challenges in terms of their ability to be politically engaged and the perception of them as women. Regarding political engagement, both stated that they were not entirely limited but that most of their political activity stemmed from their respective bishops. For example, the lay female pastoral coordinator shared that she takes direction from the bishop regarding endorsement of political propositions and dissemination of related information to the parish. When approached by parishioners or others hoping to elicit information on a political issue, she checks with the diocese's Office of Social Concern to make sure it is permissible. However, she went on to say that as a pastoral coordinator she feels politically engaged in that her Church provides opportunities for parishioners to register to vote and includes information in the bulletin on policy issues. She also spoke to how religious and lay who are not tied to the diocese are much freer to engage in social policy issues. She explained that a previous female pastoral coordinator she keeps in touch with is now much more open about her political engagement, stating, "Her Facebook page blows up all the time with social policy, whether it's about the election or immigrants or whatever. She is very free in what she is saying. She would have never been that free when she was a Pastoral Coordinator."

In speaking with the women religious sister who served as a pastoral coordinator, she expressed that she did not have to formally request permission from the bishop to engage in political activity because it came down in "abundance" from what was described as a "very politically active diocese" and the guidelines were always very clear—she would not engage if it didn't come from the diocese. She shared that as a pastoral minister she had organized activities, such as local government candidate forums at the parish. Yet, she did admit, "I'm a lot freer now. I am not working for the institutional Church. I feel free, but not in the name of my Church. I've signed petitions, supported candidates, wrote letters, and made phone calls. As a religious woman I've been to several demonstrations for gay rights."

Additionally, how these female pastoral coordinators are treated as female leaders in parishes and dioceses was also discussed. One of these challenges appears to be how the laity perceives them. Both of the pastoral coordinators explained that some parishes that did not have this administrative model before their arrival demonstrated some resistance in their ability to view the female pastoral coordinator as "in charge." The lay female pastoral coordinator described one scenario in which a parishioner questioned her upholding of her predecessor's position on an issue and expressed dissatisfaction by asking her who was in charge, to which she answered that she was, as the pastoral coordinator, via her appointment by the bishop; the parishioner insisted she was not, stating, "No, no, no, no. You're not a priest, so you can't be in charge." She shared that because she was a lay woman and not religious, she felt double "whammied" or disadvantaged in terms of being seen as an authority figure among some parishioners. She spoke of experiences when her educational credentials (she possessed a master's degree in Pastoral Theology and also an MBA) were called into question, with some congregants telling her, "You don't have the same education as a priest, you don't have the same formation."

These female pastoral coordinators also spoke of similar challenges due to their nonclerical status. As the female religious pastoral coordinator interviewed said, "People didn't quite know what to do with us. The priests didn't know what to do with us." She expressed that part of this may stem from the fact that the institutional Church does not promote females to clerical positions of leadership, so both female religious and nonreligious are in an interesting zone as pastoral coordinators; therefore, it can be difficult for the laity, priests, and even other female religious to grow accustomed to their positions of leadership. She elaborated that despite knowing many good and holy priests, the leadership was "an old boys club, and it's a very closed club, and the clericalism is rampant." For example, in light of the priest shortage and the creation of this position, both pastoral coordinators discussed how some bishops are still showing a preference for male-appointed deacons or priests from other countries to fill the leadership roles for parishes because they are part of the clergy. Furthermore, as CARA reported, the number of pastoral coordinators has decreased from a high of 553 in 2005 to 431 in 2015 (CARA 2017). Inevitably, this limits opportunities for female leadership and can create the continuation of both the hierarchy and some laity not receiving exposure to female Catholic administrative leaders. It can also have negative consequences for developing female congregants' level of political interest and participation (Djupe and Olson 2013).

The nonordained and nonclerical status of women is still inevitably a limitation, particularly for those working in the institutional Church. This was illustrated by the female religious pastoral coordinator who pointed out that while at a forum on the position, one of the attending priests showed concern that lay and female pastoral coordinators do not take a vow of obedience to a bishop in the same way ordained clergy do (i.e., deacons and priests). She also discussed how her position as nonclerical limited her liturgically serving the parish on a regular basis in terms of conducting sermons and leading worship. This example is similar to that of Wallace's (1988) finding that there was frustration among some female pastoral ministers who also felt their liturgical and overall ministerial roles were limited, despite the fact that as a result of their professional, theological, and counseling competencies, female religious are arguably more qualified than their male counterparts (Ebaugh 1993).

Ebaugh (1993) also puts this in the context of "dual labor market labor theory," in that the higher status jobs (performed in this case by the male clergy) are more rewarding, while the secondary labor sector (that of female religious) are paid less, have little authority, and offer little opportunity to move into the primary labor sector. I argue that this institutional dynamic has perpetuated a culture in which some Catholics struggle to accept and promote female leadership. Evidence for this is indicated in the interview commentary above as well as the work of Schlumpf (2011) who found women in the Church did not always have a voice, either due to their lack of a liturgical role or a dynamic in which men were naturally more respected. Furthermore, sisters working in parishes under clergy experienced more dissatisfaction due to stifled upward mobility (Wittberg 1989).

Overall, both discussions with the female pastoral coordinators shed light on the ability of women to obtain levels of administrative leadership positions within the Church while still having to navigate around the constraints imposed on them by the institution and laity. One pattern seems to be consistent across females, particularly religious, and that is those who are not tied to the institution have more freedom, autonomy, and mobility in terms of engaging in politics and impacting lay Catholic public opinion on issues. They also appear to be freer in terms of what they say as women religious as opposed to in the name of the Church. Working outside the confines of the institutional Church appears to, at times, be an advantage in impacting social change. As some female religious interviewed expressed, although supportive of female priests, they personally have no desire to be ordained at the risk of losing this freedom. One female religious stated, "You are very tied to the bishop and it can be a very problematic relationship."

Discussion and Implications: Women Religious Going Forward

Despite inevitable institutional constraints, many of the female religious interviewed stated that they did not feel inhibited in terms of making a political impact. However, those specifically from religious congregations, not those tied to the institutional Church, expressed this sentiment. It appears women religious are aware of some of the benefits that exist in not being tied to the hierarchy and can capitalize on them in terms of maneuvering around institutional constraints. However, the institutional backlash received by the LCWR and NETWORK reveals that this too does not come without scrutiny. This study also shows that part of navigating institutional constraints to influence social policy is knowing when to collaborate with the Church, as evidenced by the USCCB policy and social justice staff working committees. For example, by some women religious being party to these committees they are directly able to meet with representatives of the hierarchy and their staff and work on social policy initiatives. For instance, in addition to the Justice for Immigrants committee, the representative interviewed from the LCWR noted that she is also on two other working groups that coincide with her mission on social justice, the USCCB's Catholic Climate Covenant and the Coalition of Catholic Organizations against Human Trafficking. Here women religious are aware that the bishops have a variety of resources, and as the representative from the CMSM noted, Capitol Hill considers what comes from the USCCB as the official Church position and consensus; therefore, the sisters have a strategic interest on partnering and working with the bishops on issues that are near to their social justice mission.

This analysis also demonstrates that religious life is different than institutional life within the faith. However, religious life, similar to the ordained clergy shortage, faces its own challenges. CARA reported that there has been a 72.5 percent drop-off in women's religious orders from a high of 181,421 in 1966 to below 50,000 today. Ebaugh (1993) suggests that some of the reason for this decline is an increase of educational and professional opportunities for women and the rise of feminism.

In discussing the current state of religious life in the United States, some sisters shared that they believe there is still an impact to be made, but the structure of congregations is changing as some are merging together due to smaller numbers. Several of the female religious here shared that many religious congregations have "associate" or lay members that have become increasingly popular and work alongside the religious in their efforts. As one sister pointed out, the culture of the United States is changing; opportunities for women have increased academically and professionally. From the 1950s to the 1960s, there was a surge of sister growth from 147,310 to 181,421 by 1966 (Berrelleza et al. 2014). Several of the sisters interviewed discussed that this was the only option for Catholic women who did not feel called to marital life (see also Ebaugh 1993). Noting the contemporary cultural shifts in America, one sister stated, "Now the idea of giving your entire life is not supported, the youth are raised different, you have technology, more opportunities, shifts in jobs. Perhaps the idea of committing yourself to a religious community or mission, should be something done for several years; therefore, perhaps the notion of life giving vows will need to be re-explored." These are some of the realities for the institutional Church and religious going forward. The female religious interviewed appeared to be hopeful for the future in their abilities to continue to be politically engaged, focus on issues of social justice, work across congregations and with the laity, as well as collaborate with younger sisters entering the covenant that will not have to fight the antiquated battles of Vatican II's reform interpretation. To some extent this is what Brigham (2015) argues comprises their "counterpublics" and upholds them as models of a new Church for Catholics in the United States that is more egalitarian and publicly engaged. However, this still limits female religious leadership within the institution and official hierarchy, where one could argue this way of being "church" is needed the most.

3

Evaluating the Doctrinal Assessment

Positions, Priorities, and Mobilization Efforts

Through a content analysis of policy statements from the USCCB and the LCWR, this chapter seeks to examine some of the claims of the Doctrinal Assessment made against the LCWR. As discussed in Chapters 1 and 2, the Vatican's CDF issued a Doctrinal Assessment of the LCWR in April 2012. As highlighted in Chapter 2, there is some debate surrounding why the Assessment was issued. Some of those interviewed claim it was brought on by the nuns' support of the ACA, while others suggest it was spurred as a way for the hierarchy to flex its institutional authority and control over the nuns. Other reports suggest that the conflict between the institutional Church and groups like the LCWR had been growing since the Second Vatican Council of the 1960s, which, as previously noted, liberalized aspects of religious life in the Church. For many women religious in the United States, the reforms were interpreted as a call to return to the intentions of their congregations' founders, spurring more focus on issues of social justice and less attention on promoting and communicating Church doctrine (Neuman 2012).

Throughout the Assessment, the LCWR denied that their organization was not in line with Church teaching (Bauman 2013). The CDF claimed that materials from the LCWR and speeches given at their annual conferences were "problematic" and contained "serious theological, even doctrinal errors." The Assessment went on to address policies of corporate dissent, arguing that the LCWR had protested the Church's position on female ordination and pastoral care of homosexuals. The CDF also claimed commentaries on the patriarchy sponsored by the LCWR distorted the intention and structure of the Church (Vatican 2012). As previously mentioned, the Assessment was overseen by three member bishops of the USCCB and included a review of the LCWR's documents for a twelve-year period (2000 through 2012). Upon its conclusion, the LCWR affirmed its original position that the Assessment was not an accurate view of the organization's lived experience and that the concerns raised did not warrant the level of institutional scrutiny received (LCWR 2015).

Again, a closer look at the Assessment of the LCWR raises the issue of policy and authority within a gendered institution. According to the Church, the LCWR had a different set of priorities and positions on various social policy issues that challenged institutional authority. As women religious, the LCWR views its work as obedient to the gospel of social justice advocated by Vatican II. This perspective demonstrates the tension of institutional authority within the Church since the council, which the LCWR feels also called for a more participatory role by female religious in the decision making of the Church. Sister Pat Farrell (past president of the LCWR) shared these sentiments in an interview at the beginning stages of the Assessment process, expressing how her congregation studied Vatican II and worked to serve people at the margins of society, dealing with issues such as homelessness, AIDS, torture, and sexual trafficking. For many women religious and scholars, such as Margaret Susan Thompson, the LCWR is an example of women religious who took the council's reforms seriously and became controversial figures within the institutional Church for doing so (Berry 2012).

Moreover, Catholic female religious have invoked their own "identities and authority" by directly engaging the public, sharing their narratives and individual experiences in areas of social policy. Again, this is witnessed through recent movements such as

NETWORK's Nuns on the Bus national tours and the LCWR's traveling museum exhibit, *Women in Spirit* (Brigham 2015). Through these venues, Catholic female religious have encountered the larger public and by their stories connected "personal narratives with political issues" and by acting as "public Catholic figures, also bridged faith and political advocacy" (110). These actions by Catholic female religious demonstrate their sense of hands-on policy experience in working with the laity and the sense of authority they have drawn.

In evaluating this tension between policy and authority in a gendered institutional context, the Assessment raises the question of whether the LCWR's statements and priorities on social policy issues were in opposition to Church teaching and if the organization attempted to mobilize on these issues. To conduct this evaluation, I examine the policy statements of the LCWR and the USCCB over the period the Assessment used to analyze the nuns' publications (2000–2012). This may seem an unequal or odd comparison; however, it is important to remember that the bishops represent the official Church hierarchy in the United States and are part of its teaching and governing functions, giving rise to their authority as "authentic teachers of faith and morals" (USCCB 2017a). Furthermore, the bishops have governing authority over all religious and clergy within their diocese (*Catechism of the Catholic Church* 2010). Extrapolated, the USCCB has an interest in ensuring that religious organizations and congregations within the American Catholic Church are in line with institutional teaching, hence the bishops were delegated to oversee the renewal of the LCWR on behalf of the Vatican as prescribed by the Assessment. It can then be safely assumed that the positions of the bishops, as identified in their policy statements, are in accordance with the views of the institutional Church.

Moreover, comparing these two leadership groups, though arguably with different aims and at times audiences, gives insight into the gendered nature of the Church and the tension that exists between policy and authority. This analysis demonstrates that as women religious, the LCWR had different social policy priorities than the Church. On those issues, the LCWR felt a sense of authority due to their interpretation of Vatican II, education, professionalization, call to social justice teaching, and long history of closely working with the laity. This analysis also demonstrates that because of this tension between policy and authority, the hierarchy had some misperceptions of the LCWR, which is in line with the organization's position that the Assessment did not reflect their lived experience.

The content analysis involves these organizations' public policy statements on the economy, immigration, the death penalty, the environment, health care, homosexuality, and gender roles as both groups have a history of issuing statements on these topics. In terms of these seven social policy issues, this chapter will primarily focus on each organizations' priorities, positions, and mobilization efforts—beginning to shed light on the Assessment and evaluating its claims.

Expectations

As a result of these organizations being gender based and the criticism the nuns received from the hierarchy on some of their social stances, it seems reasonable that policy positions between the LCWR and the more socially conservative USCCB would differ. Specifically, I expect to find that these groups will have different policy positions on the topics of gender roles and homosexuality. Due to the claims of the Assessment, it is expected that the LCWR advocates a position of women religious' empowerment within the Church, and the USCCB to support more traditional gender roles. I also expect the LCWR to have a more inclusive position on homosexuality than the USCCB. However, since both organizations are of the same faith and employ elements of Catholic social teaching, they may share some similar policy positions in other areas. For example, both have a long history of speaking out on issues of a more equitable economy, less restrictive immigration policies, abolishment of the death penalty, and better stewardship of the environment.

Last, regarding mobilization, I expect both the LCWR and the USCCB to call their audiences to mobilization activities in their statements—since part of the purpose of these documents is to get their respective congregations to act on a given policy issue. I expect both groups to call more equally for mobilization on issues such as the economy, immigration, and the death penalty. However, I specifically expect to find that the USCCB will call their audience to more mobilization activity than the nuns, which may be a result of the amount of resources the bishops have compared to the LCWR. Due to the bishops' emphasis on abortion, I expect to see more calls for mobilization surrounding areas of health care.

Methodology

Using a content analysis approach to determine if these two organizations have different social policy priorities, take different policy positions, and call their congregations to mobilize, a population of 188 total statements between the two groups, over a twelve-year period from 2000 through 2012, covering the topics of the environment, homosexuality, health care, economics, the death penalty, immigration, and gender roles, was analyzed. Again, this stretch of time was chosen because it was the period of years that the CDF selected in reviewing the LCWR's documents and activities under the Assessment. The population of documents analyzed consisted of all available policy position and educational/information statements issued by both groups. For the USCCB, the statements consisted of pastoral letters, statements, bulletin inserts, action alerts, and backgrounders. Statements analyzed for the LCWR were Annual Assembly Presidential and Keynote speeches and their publication *Resolutions to Action*.

The percentage of occurrence of positions on the topics examined was calculated. By being immersed in the data pool, coders were able to identify recurring positions the organizations took on the seven topics analyzed. For example, on the topic of economics, one of the positions was whether or not the organization had statements supporting affordable housing. Out of fifty statements the USCCB had on the topic of the economy, twenty-five of them supported affordable housing; hence 50 percent of their statements on the economy included taking a stance on this position. Statements such as, "Guaranteeing affordable housing to all has been a continuing challenge . . . decent housing is a human right, its provision involves a public responsibility" (USCCB 2011) helped identify the message as fitting within the position of support for affordable housing. This same methodical process was employed for identifying positions across all topics between both organizations.

Furthermore, to determine the type of mobilization activity or call to action that the bishops or nuns called for, a hand-coding approach was again used. This assisted in identifying specific calls to action, such as petition the government, self-reflection/prayer, or a home-centered activity. The coding schemes for each topic were also constructed to aid in determining what type of mobilization these groups called for. For each topic, statements were coded regarding each of the respective organizations' attempts to mobilize their audiences via a course of action. For example, if the USCCB called for their audience to contact a member of Congress in a statement, it was coded under the "petition the government" type of mobilization category. If the USCCB asked their audience to specifically contact a "Catholic" politician, it was coded the same way. The activity of prayer/self-reflection was designed to capture if the statement called for Catholics to "pray," "read," "re-examine our own attitudes and positions," and/or "learn more about Catholic teaching." The concept of home-centered activity was constructed to capture pursuits that called people to take action at their home or local level, such as "do a personal energy audit to determine ways you can conserve" or "decide to invest in green energy through your local energy company." Last, the concept of volunteering captured language that asked the audience to either directly "volunteer" their time or take part in "sponsoring" local church events on a social issue considered. After each type of mobilization activity was accounted for, it was then divided by the total number of statements from the organization in order to arrive at a percentage of how often the USCCB called on their audience to mobilize toward a particular activity. Regarding the topic of economics, for example, the

USCCB called their audience to some type of mobilization in all fifty of their policy statements; therefore, 100 percent of their statements call for action. Out of that 100 percent (or fifty statements), forty of them specifically call to petition the government (e.g., contact their member of Congress expressing the statement/bishops' position), hence 80 percent of the statements from the USCCB on the economy call for this type of mobilization.[1]

Findings

The results of the content analysis uncovered similarities and differences between the LCWR and the USCCB. The results of each element of the research question are discussed in the sections below.

Prioritization of Topics

Table 3.1 captures the priorities of the USCCB and the LCWR.[2] The prioritization of topics was measured by the total percentage of statements each organization made on the issue. It is clear that these two organizations have different priorities in terms of the social policy issues they promote via their statements. For example, the results demonstrate that the bishops placed a premium on issues surrounding the economy and health care. Meanwhile, the LCWR focused more attention on the environment, then the economy, followed by gender roles. Though the LCWR took a position of supporting the ACA as indicated by their signing of an official letter to Congress supporting the legislation, their statements analyzed here did not indicate the issue as a priority. This may be due to nuns not having a shared concern with the bishops on issues of conscience protection, the federal funding of abortion, and reproductive care services in regard to legislation on health care. These concerns regarding health care can be seen as a priority in the USCCB's statements, such as their 2007 pastoral, *Forming Consciences for Faithful Citizenship*, along with various action alerts and informational backgrounders issued by the bishops to dioceses and parishioners during the time period analyzed.

TABLE 3.1. PRIORITIZATION OF POLICY TOPICS BY PERCENTAGE

Topic	% of USCCB Statements*	% of LCWR Statements*
Economics	40.0	25.4
Health Care	23.2	4.8
Immigration	10.4	7.9
Homosexuality	7.2	4.8
Death Penalty	7.2	3.2
Gender Roles	7.2	15.9
Environment	4.8	38.1

*Total statements per organization: USCCB, 125; LCWR, 63.

The third ranking topic for the LCWR, gender roles, also indicates a difference of priorities between the two groups. For example, 15.9 percent of the nuns' statements emphasized gender roles while only 7.2 percent did so for the USCCB; this finding is consistent with the expectations. Prioritizing gender roles may be a result of female religious not being tied to the hierarchy and hence having some flexibility to act independently of the Church and promulgate in the name of their congregation, their organization, or as individual sisters—something that may be more difficult for a diocesan priest to do (Stalp and Winders 2002). Yet, it may be a result of the female religious level of professionalization, living out Vatican II reforms and pushing for more equality in the Church.

Specific Policy Positions

Next, the actual content of the statements was coded to assess whether they are taking the same positions on the issues examined. The following section breaks down the results on the policy positions by topic, beginning with topics on which there are more similarities between the organizations and moving to those on which there is divergence. The results show that the USCCB and the LCWR have more similar positions on economics, immigration, the death penalty, and the environment. The two organizations' positions diverge on health care and differ substantially on homosexuality and gender roles.

Economics

The results in figure 3.1 show that both organizations support the position of a larger role for government in the economy. The USCCB took this position in 100 percent of their statements and the LCWR in 75 percent of theirs, which is fairly in line with expectations. Both groups also supported economic justice for the poor, addressed in 81 percent of LCWR documents and in 36 percent of USCCB statements. Other areas signal different focuses of support—the USCCB made more statements on affordable housing and to a lesser degree predatory lending, where the LCWR did not signal a position on these specific economic issues.

Immigration

As expected, both organizations took pro-immigration positions. Figure 3.2 shows that both organizations supported immigration reform (the USCCB in 54 percent and the LCWR in 80 percent of their documents). The results show that both organizations take the position of supporting a larger role of government in ensuring immigration reform (85 percent of the USCCB's documents and 60 percent of the LCWR's documents). The LCWR also emphasized support for immigration reform by reiterating the USCCB's positions. For example, "As a member of the Justice for Immigrants Campaign of the USCCB, LCWR promotes legislation that includes family reunification, a path to earned legalization, worker protections and an effective border policy that is humane rather than punitive" (LCWR 2006a).

Death Penalty

It is not surprising that the two organizations were unanimous on the death penalty, both calling for abolition in 100 percent of their statements. The USCCB (2005) states, "The sanction of death, when it is not necessary to protect society, violates respect for human life and dignity." Similarly, the LCWR states, "Abolition

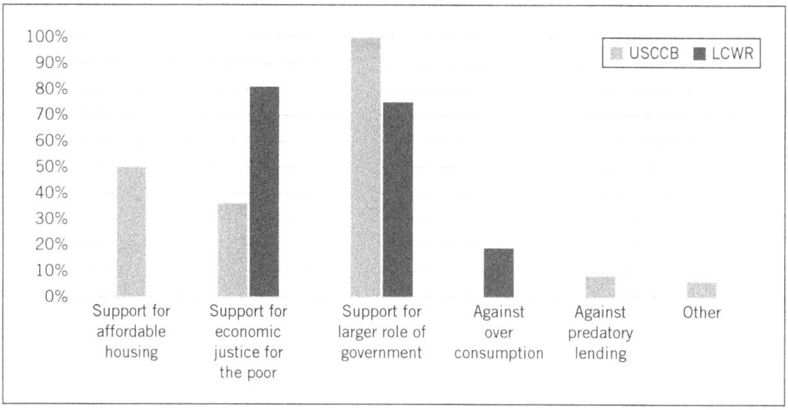

Figure 3.1. Specific economic concerns addressed in organizational statements, 2000–2012.

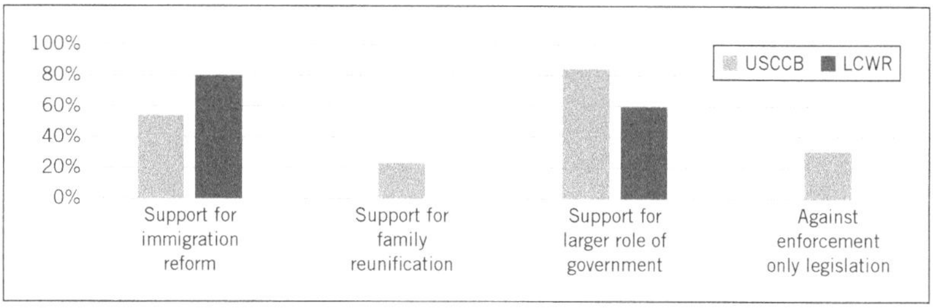

Figure 3.2. Specific immigration concerns addressed in organizational statements, 2000–2012.

of capital punishment is also a manifestation of our belief in the unique worth and dignity of each person" (Donahue 2006). These results are consistent with the expectation that both groups would similarly support the abolition of the death penalty.

Environment

As indicated in figure 3.3, the USCCB and the LCWR also have similar positions on the environment, supporting a larger role for government involvement (the USCCB 100 percent and the LCWR 83 percent). Some of the differences in the groups' positions are that the USCCB takes more of a pronounced stance in their support for addressing climate change, as seen in their

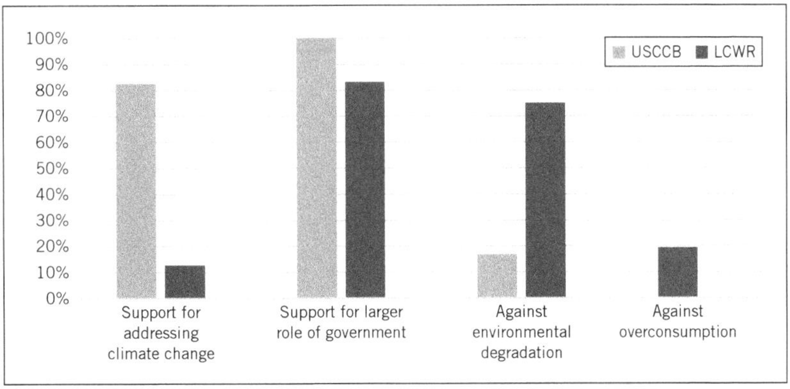

Figure 3.3. Specific environmental concerns addressed in organizational statements, 2000–2012.

having a greater percentage of statements on the topic than the LCWR (83 percent to 13 percent, respectively). Specifically, in its support for addressing climate change through their statements, the USCCB acknowledges the existence of climate change and calls for policies to reduce the negative consequences of it. In regard to the LCWR's position against environmental degradation, their statements more specifically addressed the deterioration of the environment via pollution, the depletion of resources, and the ecosystem.

Health Care

As mentioned in the introduction of this book, health care is an issue where positions and priorities between the LCWR and the USCCB begin to diverge. The bishops had the second most statements on health care (23.2 percent of the 125 documents analyzed from the organization). For the LCWR, however, the topic of health care was included in only 4.8 percent of the 63 statements examined for the nuns. Both groups demonstrate a level of support for affordable health care. The LCWR's position for affordable health care is more pronounced—their support for it is in 100 percent of their statements on the issue, where the USCCB only does so in 17 percent. The results show that the USCCB uses their statements on health care to take a position against the fed-

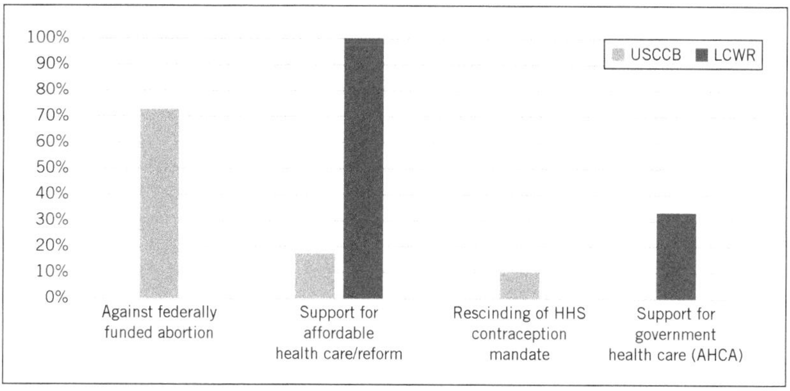

Figure 3.4. Specific health care policy concerns addressed in organizational statements, 2000–2012.

eral funding of abortion (used in 72 percent of their statements), a position the LCWR does not address in its policy pronouncements on this topic. These findings illustrate an important point of difference and concern for these two groups. For the bishops, their primary concern is rooted in the institutional pro-life position on abortion and contraception. On the other hand, having a long history in the United States as health care practitioners and providers, Catholic women religious, such as the LCWR and their affiliates, were more concerned with expanding coverage to as many people as possible. As the nuns stated in a 2010 letter to Congress supporting the ACA, "We write to urge you to case a life-affirming yes . . . we see the toll on families who have delayed seeking care due to lack of health insurance coverage or lack of funds with which to pay high deductibles and co-pays" (Catholic Medical Association 2010). (See figure 3.4.)

One can see the divergence of position on this particular health care issue in the context of the 2010 ACA, as displayed in an address at the LCWR's Annual Assembly that year: "In the end, relying on the research of its staff, the USCCB felt it could not support the final form of the healthcare reform bill because, in the conference's view, there were not adequate protections against federal funding of abortions. The LCWR, many individual women religious communities and the Catholic Health Association, supported the legislation because they believed the specific legislative protections were adequate" (Gaillardetz 2010). As previously noted, the disagreement on the ACA would prove consequential for the relationship between the LCWR and the USCCB, as several noted in the previous chapter that they believed this divide help propel the Doctrinal Assessment of the nuns.

Homosexuality

The LCWR's position on homosexuality supports the "full participation" of LGBT members and an "alternative ethic of sexuality" in the Church (Zollman 2003). This differs completely from the USCCB, which states, "There are many forces in our society that promote a view of sexuality in general, and of homosexuality in particular, not in accord with God's purpose and plan for human sexuality" (USCCB 2006).

As indicated in figure 3.5, homosexuality presents a topic where the organizations diverge sharply. All of the statements issued by the bishops advocated positions against same-sex unions, whereas 33 percent of the LCWR's statements supported full inclusion of homosexuals in the Church, and 66 percent of their statements supported an alternative sexual ethic/acceptance of same-sex relationships. It is worth noting that the LCWR does not directly call for the Church to begin performing same-sex marriages, but unlike the bishops, they advocate for the inclusion of homosexual Catholics and do not refer to their sexuality in a disordered way as the USCCB does. This position of inclusion is a major priority for the LCWR. These results are consistent with the expectations that the LCWR would have a more progressive stance on this issue.

Gender Roles

Position differences are also evident on the issue of gender roles. As expected, the LCWR takes a position that supports equal roles of women in the Church while the USCCB does not. (See figure 3.6.) The LCWR is more adamant (as shown in 80 percent of their documents) than the USCCB in support of an equal role for women in the Church, evident in the following statement: "Many of us as women, and as women religious, hold a hope and

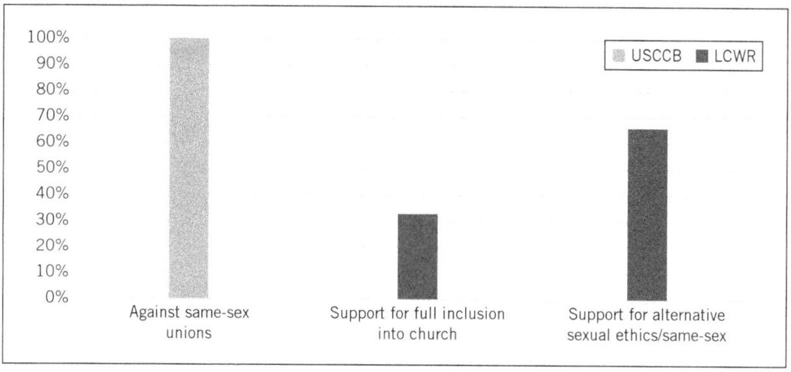

Figure 3.5. Specific positions on homosexuality addressed in organizational statements, 2000–2012.

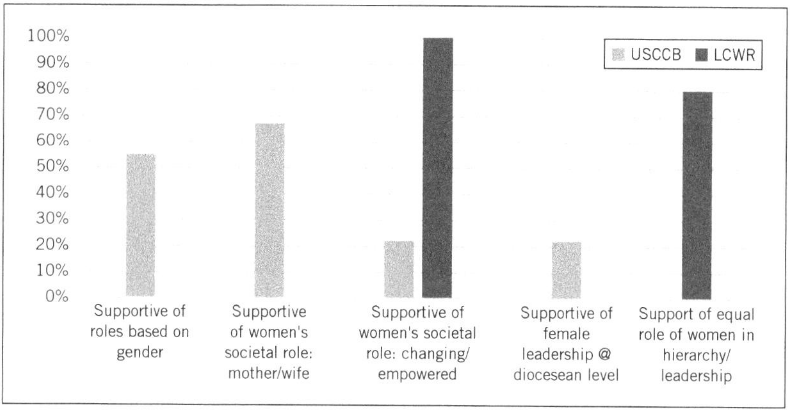

Figure 3.6. Specific positions on gender roles addressed in organizational statements, 2000–2012.

lay a claim, to a place and a voice in the Church as full participants in its life and mission because of our one baptism into the Risen Christ in whom there is not distinction of gender" (Robinson 2004). On the other hand, the USCCB supports the decision by the hierarchy of a male-only clergy.[3]

The results show the USCCB supported traditional gender roles (55 percent). The USCCB's statements about gender are fairly orthodox, for example, "The difference between man and woman, however, cannot be restricted to their bodies, as if the body could be separated from the rest of the human person" (USCCB 2009a). The LCWR seeks to empower women in the Church by making statements such as, "Women must be enabled to participate fully and equally in decision making within the faiths themselves" (Robinson 2004).

Mobilization

As the analysis above demonstrates, the LCWR and the USCCB have different priorities and, at times, diverging social policy positions, but do they call for action differently as well? The findings support that both organizations called their audiences to mobilize. Overall, in 86 percent of its total statements the USCCB called its audience to mobilization via a call to action for volunteering, self-reflection/prayer, home-centered activities, and petitioning Catholic politicians or the government (such as contacting Congress). The LCWR called its audience to these types of mobilization activities in 74 percent of their statements. Figure 3.7 gives a view of the percentage per topic of how often the USCCB and the LCWR mobilized their audiences via the activities just noted.

For the topics of environment and economics, both groups called on their audience to act in 100 percent of their policy statements. Overall, the topics in which the USCCB called for mobilization activities the most were economics, the environment, and health care. The LCWR called their audiences to mobilize most on the death penalty, the economy, and the environment. The two main differences between the organizations were in the topics of health care and homosexuality. In both of these topics the LCWR did not call its audience to a particular activity. This finding coincides with some of the points cited in the Doctrinal Assessment of the LCWR, which reprimanded the group for its silence on abortion and homosexuality. In contrast, the USCCB called its audience to act 22 percent of the time in its statements on homosexuality and 100 percent in its statements on health care. This latter result is not necessarily surprising since many of

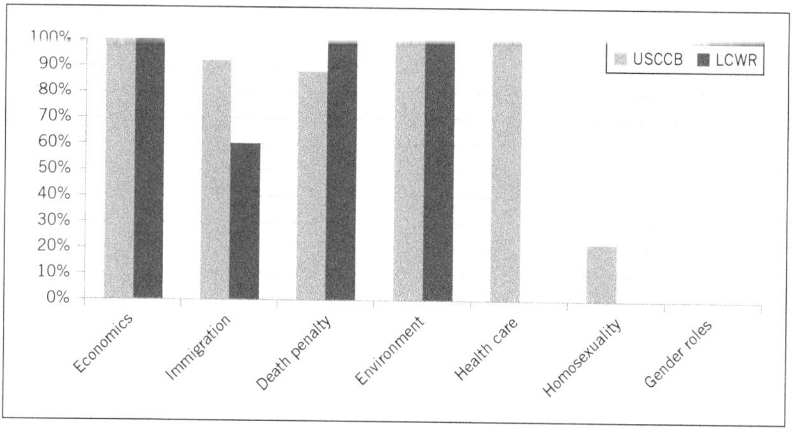

Figure 3.7. Total percentages of mobilization activities called for across topics in organizational statements, 2000–2012.

the bishops' statements on health care during the time period analyzed were concerned with the potential of health care reform to be tied to federally funded abortion, contraception mandates, and issues of conscience protection for health care providers. Again, these right-to-life issues for the bishops lie at the heart of their teaching and have been considered their number one policy and political rallying point (Waggoner 2008; Sunshine 1989). However, another issue that the LCWR did not mobilize on was issues of gender, which is counter to the Assessments claims of radical feminism. One would think that if the LCWR was pushing an extreme feminist ideology that they would be calling their audience to mobilize around it, which is not observed here—signaling a misconception by the Assessment.

Figure 3.8 shows what specific mobilization type of activities were suggested the most by each organization across all topics considered. The results demonstrate that "petition the government" was the mobilization activity employed the most (54 percent of the bishops' messages and 30 percent of the LCWR's messages).

Both organizations called for their audiences to engage in self-reflection and prayer on the seven topics; the USCCB did this in 26 percent of their statements and the LCWR in 16 percent of theirs. The main differences tended to be in volunteering, calling

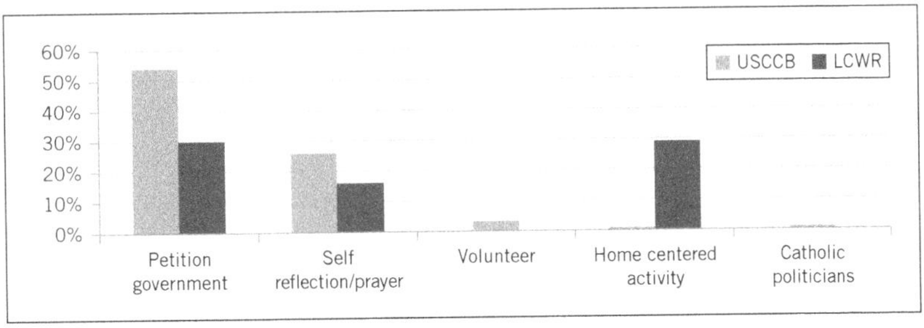

Figure 3.8. Overall percentage of organizational statements calling for each mobilization activity type, 2000–2012.

on Catholic politicians to adhere to Church teachings, and home-centered activity. In the former two, the LCWR employs these mobilization calls less than 1 percent of the time. However, regarding home-centered activity, the LCWR employs this mobilization technique in 29 percent of their policy statements, most of which center on the environment. This call for home-centered activity from the LCWR may be due to a more prominent female socialization in the domestic sphere. Also, the LCWR suggests ways to be more environmentally conscience at home, perhaps in an attempt to get their audience to take practical, everyday steps in this direction and in their own lives.

Conclusion and Implications

The results indicate that the USCCB and the LCWR share commonalities on most policy topics. Differences lie in the prioritization of topics and the degree to which positions are emphasized. For example, both groups held economics as a top priority (number one for the USCCB and second for the LCWR), but the LCWR focused on economic justice for the poor and the USCCB emphasized affordable housing; however, both groups largely agreed on the stance of having a larger government role in the economy. The bishops and the nuns also both favored a larger role of the government regulating the environment; however, this topic was a much higher priority for the LCWR than the USCCB. Both groups also called for abolition of the death penalty and immigration reform.

Interestingly, on these issues the Vatican has demonstrated fairly similar positions, either via papal encyclicals, apostolic letters, or other official statements. Therefore, both groups appear to be in line with Church positions and teachings on these issues.

Their positions begin to diverge on health care, with the USCCB showing more concern for their position against federally funded abortion than the LCWR. However, what was not in disagreement was both groups' position supporting affordable health care, although the LCWR did address this particular position in more of their statements than the bishops, and which arguably propelled their support of the ACA of 2010, as discussed in the previous chapter. The Vatican has also emphasized a similar position to that of the LCWR on health care in arguing that it is an inalienable right that should be accessible (Vatican 2009). This may be what is at the heart of the Church's claim that the LCWR was "silent" on issues of abortion and the false perception by the hierarchy may simply be rooted in a difference of priorities. For example, in none of the LCWR's statements do they advocate for abortion nor do they mobilize on the issue. However, as some of the nuns specified in the previous chapter, it is not the only pro-life issue for them and many other social justice issues are. This coupled with the fact that bishops do make abortion such a significant priority in their statements on health care, especially that they do not want it to be federally funded, is where one of the conflicts lies. It appears that the bishops and the Church equate the LCWR's silence on the issue with supporting it; however, there is no evidence to suggest that.

The two groups also diverged on issues of homosexuality and gender roles. Regarding the former, the LCWR supported a more open view of homosexuality, yet again, this was not an issue they mobilized on. Regarding the gender roles, the bishops concentrate on more traditional roles of women and only permit them to have certain diocesan leadership positions (which too is consistent with prior official Vatican positions, as seen in *Ordinatio Sacerdotalis*).[4] Meanwhile, the LCWR supports a more empowered role for women across the hierarchy as evidenced in the interview chapter, but they are not calling for mobilization activity on this issue, again challenging the claims of "radical feminism" by the Doctrinal Assessment. Furthermore, what is an interesting recent development on the issue of women's empowerment in the Church is that after meeting with women leaders in the Church, Pope Francis has commenced a commission to look at the possibility of a female diaconate (Green 2016). There is a debate as to whether the female diaconate will be the same as the permanent male diaconate that came out of Vatican II, which is an ordained and clerical position. Per the interviews with women religious for this study, some discussed it is a positive and empowering step forward for women in the Church.

However, it is apparent that the organizations have more positions in common than those on which they diverge. Perhaps the idea behind the Assessment is that the LCWR does not emphasize certain orthodox views of the Church to the same degree as the hierarchy. The conservative and progressive (or social justice) divide can be very much witnessed in the Catholic Church since Vatican II, where some argue, religious groups and even the laity interpreted the reforms too liberally (Reese 2016). Some interviewed for this study noted how the Doctrinal Assessment itself was authorized under a conservative pope, Benedict XVI, and concluded by a more social justice–oriented counterpart, Pope Francis, whose background as a Jesuit is more rooted in this approach. Again, one of the criticisms of the LCWR by the Church was its focus on social justice issues as opposed to what the hierarchy feels are more critical issues like abortion. However, the bishops discuss social justice in topics like immigration, the death penalty, and the economy, as does the LCWR. This strengthens the argument that the critical issue of the Assessment is not that the LCWR is opposed to the teachings of the Church but instead that it is not as vocal on key priorities of the hierarchy.

4

Evaluating the Claims of the Doctrinal Assessment Continued

Frames and Language Styles of the LCWR and USCCB's Policy Statements

The work began in Chapter 3 of examining some of the claims of the Doctrinal Assessment of the LCWR continues in this chapter with an analysis and comparison of the frames and language style they employ in their statements to those used by the USCCB. Do the language used and the frames employed by these organizations add to the belief that the LCWR and their policy statements were in conflict with the Church? While taking a stance on an issue is one way to connect with an audience, it is perhaps just as or more important to use the right language to convey that support. The use of a particular language style, such as the technical terminology that would appeal to an engineer, is one way audiences assess a shared identity and credibility. But particular frames (or points of emphasis) also matter as a way to connect with broader values or attitudes that can build support.

Even though religious elites' primary role is not as political actors, their function as community leaders places them in a position to take on public and social policy issues (Olson, Crawford, and Deckman 2005). Therefore, religious leaders can be viewed as vehicles of political communication, helping make sense of related issues as an extension of their roles (Campbell 2004; Djupe and

Calfano 2014; Djupe and Gilbert 2002; Smidt and Schaap 2009; Smidt et al. 2008). This dynamic can be analyzed through policy-related statements religious leaders publish (Djupe and Calfano 2014; Djupe and Gilbert 2002; Guth et al. 1997; Olson, Guth, and Guth 2003; Wald 1992). Moreover, religious language can serve an important function in influencing political behavior (McLauglin and Wise 2014); therefore, it should not be surprising that these leaders often devise policy statements on social issues they have prioritized. Scholars argue that framing can influence both religious and nonreligious choices on social policy issues (Chaves and Montgomery 1996). Furthermore, Snarr (2009) suggests that the use of language and frames by religious actors in their social policy activities are part of an intentional moral persuasion effort. Therefore, in studying policy statements of religious organizations, it is important to include a discussion on the language and various frames used.

It is important to note that frames and language style are two different things. Frames refer to themes and points of emphasis that focus on subsets or characteristics of information (Druckman 2001a and 2001b; Snarr 2009). For example, if an organization is putting out public statements calling for criminal justice reform, they may employ frames that focus on the theme of racial bias in the system, attempting for this aspect to be more prominently considered by their audience when constructing their positions. On the other hand, looking at language style entails examining the specific word choice and tone used in the statements which can signal how language is used by these groups (Bligh, Merolla, and Schroedel 2010). For example, government agencies may use more bureaucratic language, employing technical jargon that is placid, void of emotion, instructive, and likened to language one would find in a policy manual.

In proceeding with the chapter, the first part outlines the frames, related expectations, and the hand-coding content analysis approach; it then moves to a presentation of the frame findings. The second part then discusses the language style categories used, along with how the computerized assisted text analysis program, DICTION was implemented, moving to the language style findings. The chapter concludes with a discussion on the implications for the frame and language style analyses.[1] Overall, the frames and language styles used by these groups show us the differences in how they attempt to connect with the public and their congregations. For example, the bishops employ more orthodox and mobilizing language in their statements than the nuns. And, at times, the USCCB also uses different frames, turning more focus on the topic of health care to conscience protection than the nuns, whose focus on the issue is more about vulnerable populations, such as women and children.

Frames

Why is it important to consider how these organizations frame their statements? Well, both organizations may take similar positions on issues, but the frames they use may be what causes tension between the nuns and the hierarchy. For example, the sisters may employ different frames based on their expertise and thus authority they feel they have on certain social policy issue. For example, as noted above, the findings show that the sisters frame their statements on health care with little attention to conscience protection and more focus on women and children. Regarding the topic of gender roles, the sisters employ a frame that gives more attention to female religious leadership in the Church; meanwhile the bishops focus more on natural law and how it pertains to gender roles of lay female and male Catholics.

The following discussion specifies the main frames employed by the USCCB and LCWR. The frames that emerged most frequently from the text either on a specific topic or more generally across the topics are considered. Not all frames were used universally across the statements and some were employed in more than one topic (e.g., the frame human life and dignity is used in statements on immigration and the death penalty by both organizations). The discussion below serves to first define the frames and provide expectations for how each respective organization uses them. This is then immediately followed by a presentation and discussion of the framing results. After the findings on the frames are presented, I then move to a discussion and analysis of the language styles employed by these groups.

Ecological Feminism

Ecological feminism combines the demands of the women's and ecological movements, fostering a perspective that is founded on socioeconomic and conceptual structures of domination. The common thread is the idea that the domination of women and nature are connected and mutually reinforcing (King 1989; Warren and Cheney 1991). This frame relates to the position of the LCWR on the environment, and it aids in signaling the nature of their support on how environmental degradation affects vulnerable populations, specifically women and children. The Church is critical of the LCWR's feminist views; thus, the incorporation of this frame may help identify if these female religious leaders relate and emphasize environmental issues to gender.

Conscience Protection

Conscience protection is a frame considered in relation to health care and can signal if these organizations emphasize it in their stances. Conscience protection is the right of health care providers to decline involvement in abortion, abortion referrals, administration of contraception, or involvement with any other practice that they feel violates their conscience (USCCB 2009b). We can find evidence of the USCCB's concern for this in their statement on the Health and Human Services Contraception Mandate: "The now-finalized rule of the U.S. Department of Health and Human Services that would force virtually all private health plans nationwide to provide coverage of sterilization and contraception—including abortifacient drugs . . . creates still a third class, those with no conscience protection at all: individuals who, in their daily lives, strive constantly to act in accordance with their faith and moral values" (USCCB 2012a). Further, Fogel and Rivera (2003) argue that health care providers get tied up in the conscience protection debate, making this concept important to consider. I expect that the USCCB will employ a greater percentage of the conscience protection frame in their statements than the LCWR.

Human Life and Dignity

Human life and dignity is a frame concerning immigration and the death penalty. The Catholic position on dignity for human life is not limited to abortion but spans to groups of marginalized peoples and can signal positions on immigration and the death penalty. On immigration the bishops state, "We the bishops of the United States reaffirm the commitment of the Church, in the words of Pope John Paul II, to work 'so that every person's dignity is respected, the immigrant is welcomed as a brother or sister'" (USCCB 2000). Regarding the Church's position supporting life from conception to natural death, the bishops have stated, "The life and dignity of every person must be respected and protected at every stage and in every condition" (USCCB 2010b). I expect to find that both groups utilized this frame in advocating their pro-immigration and abolition of the death penalty positions.

Natural Law

Natural law is a frame that is unique to the issues of homosexuality and gender roles, because they are the only topics that lend themselves to the Church's position on this concept and they can signal insight into the organizations' stances on these issues. The *Catechism of the Catholic Church* states, "The natural law is immutable, permanent throughout history. . . . It is a necessary foundation for the erection of moral rules and civil law. . . . The natural law, the Creator's very good work, provides the solid foundation on which man can build the structure of moral rules to guide his choices." Cardinal Timothy Dolan, president of the USCCB, reiterated, "Natural law is a concept of objective truth, not religious preference" (Griffin 2012). I expect to find that the USCCB utilizes natural law in their opposition to issues such as same-sex marriage and in their support for more traditional gender roles based on sex.

Catholic Social Teaching

There are some concept frames that encompass more general topics related to Catholic social teaching and times when both organizations reference this phrase/terminology specifically. For example, both the LCWR and USCCB discuss Catholic social teaching in terms of serving as a guide or set of instructions on various social policies. For this analysis the frame was considered when directly being referenced or when referenced in regard to specific teachings of the Church, as well as when connecting Catholic social teaching to solidarity with certain groups, advocating the need for responsible social welfare policy and stewardship. Fogel and Rivera (2003) argue that to reinforce guiding principles the Church employs Catholic social teaching directives in their policy promulgations. As part of the official teaching arm of the Church, I expect to find that the USCCB uses this concept frame more than the LCWR.

Population

In reading through the policy statements, it became evident that the LCWR and USCCB focus their attention on certain populations. Schneider and Ingram (1993) state, "The social construction of target populations refers to the cultural characterizations or popular images of the persons or groups whose behavior and well-being are affected by public policy . . . target populations has a powerful influence on public officials and shapes both the policy agenda and the actual design of policy" (334–335). Looking at the target populations can help signal the focus of the organizations' promulgation. Overall, I expect that both organizations will target vulnerable populations (such as women and children, the poor, and immigrants). However, I expect that the LCWR will focus more than the USCCB on the population of women and children in their statements.

Framing Results

The frames discussed directly above emerged from the text of the statements and were added to the coding schemes. As mentioned in the previous chapter, I coded the entire corpus of statements first. Then to gauge intercoder reliability, two trained research coders independently coded the entire sample. If a statement included one of the frames it was tallied as "1" and if it did not, "0." Once all the documents were coded, a Cronbach's Alpha test was conducted and reported a result of 0.759, which demonstrated the reliability of the coding. Overall, these frames help assess the LCWR and USCCB's statements by more clearly identifying if they focus on different themes and communicate their promulgations differently. Below are the results.

Economics

As discussed in the prior chapter, LCWR and USCCB both placed a high priority on economic issues and have fairly similar positions supporting a larger role of government in the economy. The results in figure 4.1 also show similarities between the organizations across frames. Figure 4.1 indicates both organizations addressed Catholic social teaching in their economic statements 100 percent of the time. Issues of economic equity and justice are part of the Church's social teaching, and therefore it is not surprising that both organizations use this theme/frame in their statements. For example, the LCWR has stated, "Catholic social tradition maintains that civil authority ultimately exists to achieve the common good . . . we need to focus our political will to make domestic economic justice a priority. . . . decisions must be judged in light for what they do for the poor" (Dwyer, Pinkerton, and Clark 2008, 2).

Similarly, the USCCB utilized the frame of Catholic social teaching in their position for economic justice, stating, "The Gospel and Catholic social teaching place our service of the poor and vulnerable and our work for justice at the center. . . . Government action is necessary to help overcome structures of injustice" (USCCB 2002). Both of these statements convey similar points

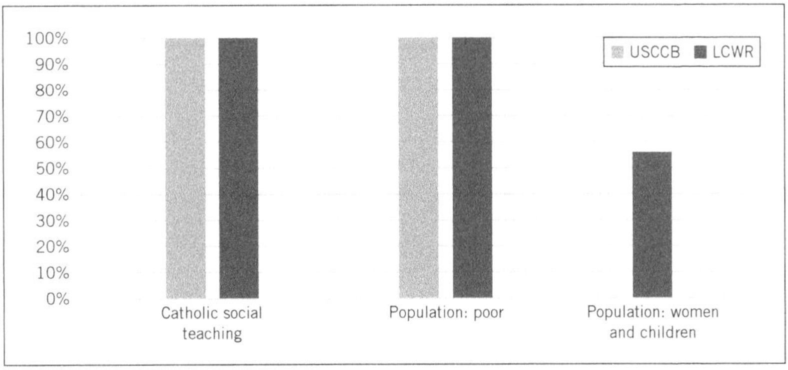

Figure 4.1. Economic frames used in organizational statements, 2000–2012.

on the need to care for the poor and the government's responsibility to ensure that this population is served. The only differences within this issue lie in that the LCWR focused specifically on women and children.

Immigration

In Chapter 3, the findings demonstrated that both organizations support immigration reform. Here the results show that the LCWR and USCCB employ similar frames on this issue as well. Both groups focus predominantly on the immigrants themselves (the USCCB 62 percent, and the LCWR 80 percent) along with other vulnerable populations, such as women and children (the USCCB 23 percent, and the LCWR 20 percent). As expected, both groups utilize Catholic social teaching in support of their immigration reform positions (the USCCB 54 percent, and the LCWR 60 percent). (See figure 4.2.)

Death Penalty

The previous chapter also demonstrated that the bishops and nuns both supported the abolition of the death penalty in 100 percent of their documents. Both groups universally use the themes of human life and dignity, along with Catholic social teaching in framing

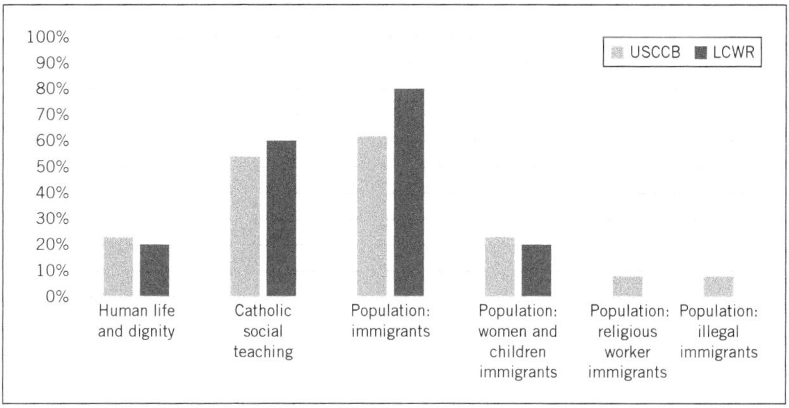

Figure 4.2. Immigration frames used in organizational statements, 2000–2012.

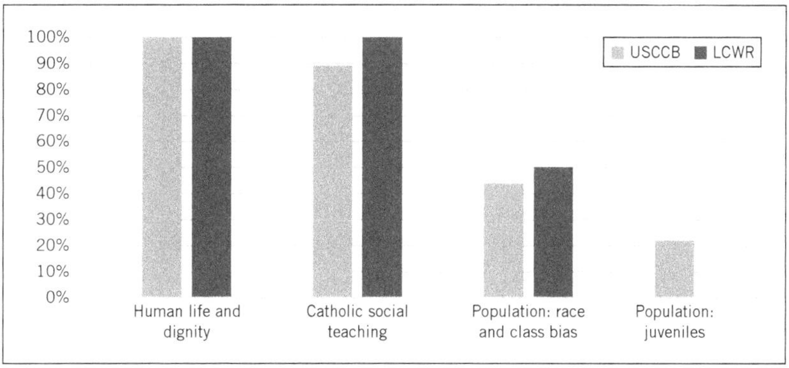

Figure 4.3. Death penalty frames used in organizational statements, 2000–2012.

their arguments against the death penalty. Moreover, both target the race and class bias (44–50 percent), however, the USCCB also places some emphasis on juveniles facing the death penalty (22 percent) whereas the LCWR does not. (See figure 4.3.)

Environment

Recalling Chapter 3, the environment was the highest priority in terms of number of policy statements for the LCWR compared to the USCCB, where it was its lowest. However, both had similar

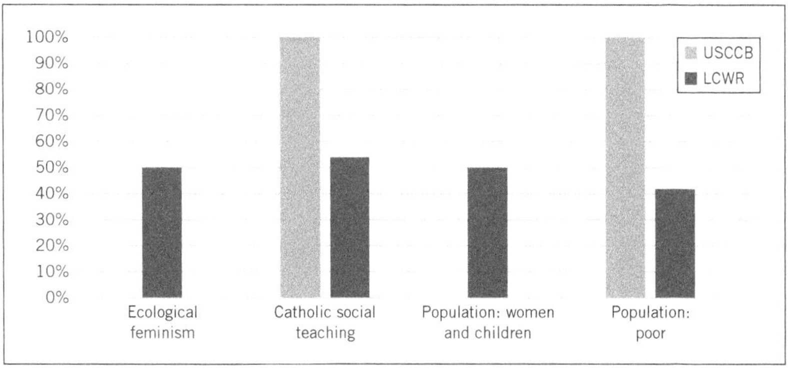

Figure 4.4. Environmental frames used in organizational statements, 2000–2012.

positions in supporting a larger role of government in regulation and protection of the environment. Yet, they also differ substantially in how they talk about the environment that shines a bright light on their organizational approaches. For example, the LCWR focuses on ecological feminism in addressing the environment (50 percent compared to 0 percent for the bishops). I argue that the nuns are more in tune with how issues, like environment degradation, can negatively impact women more than men, particularly in the developing world, making them more vulnerable and forcing them to live in refugee camps with below minimum standards of living (LCWR 2009). In turn, this type of focus in the nuns' statements (as opposed to attention on the bishops' priorities) may add to the Church's claims of radical feminism as noted in the Assessment, with the institutional position that the sisters are too focused on female empowerment and causes. (See figure 4.4.)

Health Care

The previous chapter demonstrated that health care was an issue where the two groups begin to diverge. Health care was a higher priority for the bishops. Although they took a position of supporting affordability, they addressed this stance in fewer statements than the LCWR. The results in figure 4.5 demonstrate that the

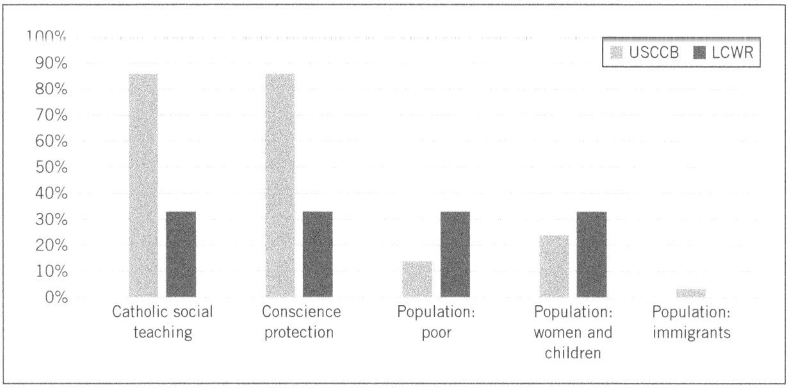

Figure 4.5. Health care frames used in organizational statements, 2000–2012.

major differences between the groups on this issue can be showcased in how they frame the health care debate. For example, the bishops emphasize Catholic social teaching and conscience protection much more in their statements than the nuns (86 percent to 33 percent, respectively). This is in part related to the concern the bishops have had over any possibility of federal money supporting abortion procedures or contraception in health care. This was not an area of focus for the LCWR and hence their statements did not include these frames. In terms of population, the LCWR does target women and children more than the USCCB. This may be the result of the nuns being more cognizant of how issues of health care impact this group more profoundly, as women and children tend to access the health care system more than men (Owens 2008). Furthermore, the LCWR also highlight the plight of the poor.

Homosexuality

As noted previously, both the USCCB and the LCWR have different priorities and, in some senses, positions on homosexuality. Homosexuality was a higher priority for the USCCB in their statements and they did not support full inclusion in the Church as the LCWR did. The groups also differ in terms of how they frame these issues. First, the USCCB uses the frame of natural law 100 percent of the time in expressing their position against homosexuality, whereas the LCWR only references it 33 percent of the time in their statements. In terms of natural law, the LCWR speaks out against the use of this frame with regard to homosexuality. For example, as past president, Mary Ann Zollman stated at an Annual Assembly address, "During one meeting, our conversation turned to a discussion of the church's position on homosexuality. As some of the participants made their appeal to ethical directives based in natural law and the intrinsically disordered nature of homosexuality, I found myself tapping into a place of grief and alienation" (2003). This differs from the USCCB, which states, "the Catholic Church has consistently taught that homosexual acts are contrary to natural law" or that "homosexual acts cannot fulfill the natural ends of human sexuality" (USCCB 2006). The LCWR focuses on the negative impact of the natural law view toward homosexuality, where the USCCB uses this frame to emphasize that homosexuality is not in accord with the nature of God's plan.

Gender Roles

As discussed in the previous chapter, gender roles are also where these two organizations have different priorities and positions. The LCWR had a higher percentage of their statements on gender roles than the USCCB and took a position of supporting a more empowered role for women in the Church. Figure 4.6 shows that the two groups also employ different frames in their positions. For example, the LCWR specifically targets women religious in their statements more than the USCCB (80 percent compared to 22 percent, respectively). However, they also discuss the male clergy more in their promulgations than the USCCB (70 percent to 33 percent, respectively). This may be a result of the USCCB's statements having more focus on the gender roles of lay men and women in the family and society, compared to the nuns. For example, the USCCB focuses on the natural institution of marriage in some of their statements and how it is "ordered" for "procreation and education" of children, carving out the distinct roles of mothers and fathers (USCCB 2009a). On the other hand, the LCWR focuses more on male and female religious' role in the

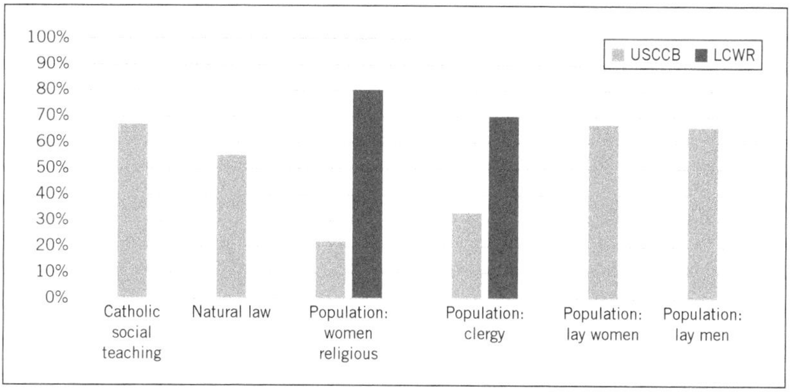

Figure 4.6. Gender role frames used in organizational statements, 2000–2012.

institutional Church. This could also be where some of the tension with authority between the male clergy and women religious comes to the head, as the LCWR in their statements and Annual Assembly speeches turn into an intrachurch group, advocating for their empowerment and advancement.

Language Styles

The CATA program DICTION was used to determine the language style of these organizations. DICTION has the ability to highlight the language style and tone of political-oriented messages. Variables from this language analysis program were used in determining the language style the USCCB and LCWR employed in their messages. However, it is also important to remember that the texts being analyzed here are from religious leadership groups and that DICTION has been used in previous studies to identify and examine religious language by both political candidates and religious leaders (Bligh, Kholes, and Meindl 2004; Bligh, Merolla, and Schroedel 2010; Hart and Lind 2011). DICTION has also been used to analyze statements and speeches used by religious groups (Eidenmuller 2002; Kraybill 2016).

DICTION 6.0 uses a computerized approach in determining the tone of verbal messages by searching passages for five general semantic features ("certainty," "activity," "optimism," "realism," and "commonality"), as well as thirty-five subfeatures or variables. The program engages in searches via a "10,000-word corpus" and specializes in identifying politically oriented speech (DICTION 6.0 Help Manual 2012). The preformulated dictionaries in the program focus on identifying the most frequently used words in American public discourse (Hart 1984). Therefore, it is an appropriate computer coding system to analyze social policy statements (Bligh, Kholes, and Meindl 2004). DICTION allows the researcher to combine variables together so that unique categories can be made to examine language. As explained below, for this analysis DICTION variables were combined in order to examine the USCCB and LCWR for specific language: feminine language, masculine language, religious language, progressive worldviews, orthodox worldviews, and mobilization language.

Feminine Language and Masculine Language

Women have been found to be more relationship oriented in their personalities and communication, expressing concern for collectives and having cooperation and passivity with others (Bligh, Merolla, and Schroedel 2010; Lipman-Bluman and Tickamyer 1975; Sell, Griffith, and Wilson 1993; Dodson and Carroll 1991; Kathleen 1994; Rosenthal 1998; Thomas, 1997). Therefore, the DICTION variables used to create feminine language were "passivity," "cooperation," "collectives," "praise," "satisfaction," and "human interest." On the other hand, scholars note that men look to stand out from others, embracing competition and forceful action, using more "I"-centered language and expressing confidence (Bligh, Merolla, and Schroedel 2010; Shapiro and Mahajan 1986; Lipman and Tickamyer 1975; Lenney 1977). Therefore, I use a different set of DICTION variables to distinguish masculine speech, such as "aggression," "accomplishment," "self-reference," and "tenacity."

Religious Language

Leaders use language that appeals to audiences' values and morals (Awamleh and Gardner 1999). Building on the work of Bligh,

Merolla, and Schroedel (2010) the variable used to examine religious language is based on the DICTION 6.0 variable "inspiration." This concept identifies terms that include abstract virtues that deserve respect, desirable moral qualities such as faith, honesty, self-sacrifice, and moral virtue. As Bligh and coauthors note, this type of language centers on values and issues of morality in order to get followers to agree with the moral authority of the leader's/messenger's positions.

Orthodox Worldview and Progressive Worldview

DICTION 6.0 also includes variables that identify language oriented with orthodox and progressive worldviews. Language that is analogous to an orthodox worldview affirms traditional mainstream tenets and has a value system rooted in transcendent and outside authority (French 2002; Hunter 1991; Hodges 2005). The DICTION variables used to formulate the language variable/category orthodox worldview are "insistence," which looks at language geared toward a preference for a limited, ordered world; "temporal awareness," which identifies terms that fix a person, idea, or event within a set time and signal concrete patterns; "centrality," which analyzes language that denotes institutional regularities, core values, designation of legitimacy, orthodoxy, decorum, congruence, and universality; and last, "certainty," which looks for terms that indicate resoluteness, inflexibility, and completeness (DICTION 6.0 Help Manual 2012; Hodges 2005; Hunter 1991; French 2002).

DICTION 6.0 also has variables that identify language oriented with a progressive worldview, which is rooted in a progressive ethos, unfolding reality, and challenging traditional paradigms (Hunter 1991; Hodges 2005). The DICTION 6.0 variables that make up this construct concept are "diversity," identifying words that describe individuals or groups of individuals who deviate from societal norms, and "liberation," which codes terms that maximize individual choice, autonomy, open-mindedness, and rejection of social conventions (DICTION 6.0 Help Manual 2012).

Mobilization-Oriented Language

The DICTION 6.0 variables that were combined to develop the category of mobilization were "activity," "optimism," and "communication." These variables were chosen to form the category of mobilization for several reasons. First, the variable "activity" identifies language that features the implementation of ideas, movement, or change. The variable "optimism" identifies language that endorses some person, group, concept, or event. Last, the variable "communication" highlights terms that refer to social interaction and social actors, such as spokespersons, preachers, and advocates, and purposes, such as rebukes, hints, responses, and persuasion (DICTION 6.0 Help Manual 2012). All of the variables that are combined to develop the category of mobilization also relate to the literature on mobilization covered in the previous chapter, as well as religious leaders' ability to influence and mobilize their audiences.

Language Style Results

Language Style of Policy Statements

The analysis of language style examines the percentage that each variable was used by the LCWR and USCCB in their overall statements. All the variables' frequency scores for each topic were tallied and then divided by the total word frequency score for all the documents by that organization. For example, the total USCCB reported DICTION 6.0 frequency word score for the language variable orthodox worldview was 23,494.39 and the total reported frequency score for all the words used in the bishops' statements on all seven topics was 228,402; therefore, the bishops deployed "orthodox worldviews" 10 percent of the time. Below are the results of the language style variables used in these organizations' overall statements.

Though the percentages in figure 4.7 are low, signaling that the framing of issues is more pronounced for both groups, the illustration still provides interesting results on the type of language

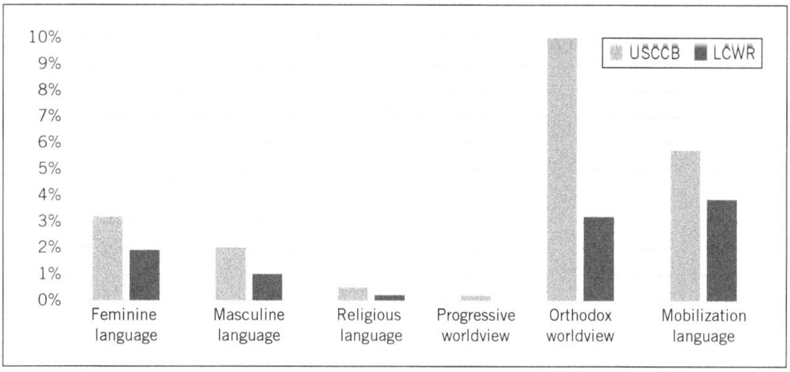

Figure 4.7. Language styles used across organizational statements, 2000–2012.

these groups use. These results highlight that both groups used mobilization language in their statements, but not often. Again, this language category was derived from the DICTION variables, "activity," "optimism," and "communication." The USCCB uses this type of language more (5.74 percent to 3.85 percent, respectively). Furthermore, the USCCB also used more orthodox language in their policy statements than the LCWR (10 percent to 3.2 percent). It is important to recall some of the DICTION variables that make up "orthodox worldviews." For example, one is the variable "centrality," which looks at terms denoting institutional regularities, agreement on values, designations of legitimacy (orthodox, decorum), ritualistic language, regularities, congruence and conformity. Another is "temporal awareness," which is indicative of language that is fixed and signals patterns and regularities in language and "certainty," which encompasses language that is inflexible and resolute.

It seems intuitive that the USCCB would use a higher percentage of orthodox language in their documents compared to the LCWR due to their institutional structure, fixed terminology and beliefs in concepts such as natural law. However, it should not be surprising that the nuns utilized more orthodox language in their statements since they employed reference to the bishops and Catholic social teaching in a variety of their messages. This scenario took place in the LCWR's January 2008, *Resolution to*

Action Publication when the group discussed economic social justice and emphasized the USCCB's pastoral, *Economic Justice for All*. However, it is clear that the LCWR does employ this type of language at a lesser percentage than the USCCB, once again indicating that some of the differences between the two organizations may come down to a matter of style and emphasis.

Despite the fact that the USCCB employed more of both masculine and feminine language, the difference in percentages used between the two groups is not wide. Overall, the USCCB employed more feminine language (3.2 percent) than masculine language (2.0 percent) in their statements. Perhaps this should not be surprising when looking more closely at what language comprises the construct variable of *feminine language* [such as "collectives" ("we"-oriented language), "raise" (affirmation of groups/persons), "passivity" (appeasement, submission), and "human interest" (which focuses on human beings and their activities and this is consistent with the communitarian approach the Catholic Church is known for)]. It may also not be unexpected that the USCCB uses a feminine language style because the Catholic faith often refers to the Church in female terms, even calling the institution "her." Christ is considered the bridegroom of the Church. As the *Catechism of the Catholic Church* states, "The theme of Christ as Bridegroom of the Church was prepared for by the prophets and announced by John the Baptist . . . Christ loved the Church and gave himself up for her, that he might sanctify her."

Overall, both the USCCB and the LCWR employ styles of language that are more orthodox and feminine, and hence "Catholic." The USCCB employs more of these styles across all of the topics analyzed, especially orthodox views. This somewhat diverges from the earlier stated expectations. For example, it was expected that the USCCB would employ more masculine language since it is a male-dominated organization, but, perhaps because of its more compassionate rhetoric toward vulnerable populations, it uses more feminine-oriented language than was assumed. However, the USCCB employs more orthodox worldviews in their language, signaling terminology that is more in line with convention. This is not surprising since the bishops are part of a conventional, hierarchical institution known for its conservative views and language. Surprisingly, neither organization employed significant amounts of religious language (the USCCB used slightly more than the LCWR); however, it may be hypothesized that the orthodox worldviews are picking up the constructs that may appear religious.

Conclusion and Implications

This chapter set out by asking if the frames and language style the USCCB and LCWR employed in their statements were different and, if so, what it might suggest about the claims of the Doctrinal Assessment. Once again, on the topics of the economy, immigration, and the death penalty, the differences in frame usage are not pronounced between the two groups. For example, on these issues, both groups frame their statements in terms of Catholic social teaching, a focus on the poor, and respect for human life and dignity. However, differences among the frames these organizations use exist across the topics of the environment, health care, homosexuality, and gender roles. All of these latter issues (less the environment) are also where differences were noted in terms of LCWR and USCCB's priorities and positions as discussed in Chapter 3. For example, on the topic of the environment, the LCWR focused more on a theme of ecological feminism, tying together how issues of environmental degradation can uniquely lead to negative consequences for women and children, whereas the USCCB concentrated more on Catholic social teaching in terms of stewardship for the environment. On the issue of health care, the bishops yield much more focus to the frame of conscience protection, while the LCWR focused instead on women's health. In terms of homosexuality, the bishops employed the natural law frame more, which is consistent with their focus on the ordered nature of human sexuality. Similarly, they used natural law as a focus in terms of gender roles, specifically in terms of the role of the family and procreation, where the LCWR focused more of its attention on women religious.

Therefore, it appears that in particular on issues of the environment, health care, homosexuality, and gender, how these groups frame their messages may add to the belief that the LCWR took or at least emphasized different positions from the Church. In terms of homosexuality, the LCWR does not employ nor put strong focus on the natural law frame like the USCCB. Regarding gender roles, the LCWR does focus more of its attention on female religious in the Church compared to the USCCB.

Furthermore, both employ similar language styles; however, the bishops utilize much more orthodox terms and slightly more mobilization language than the LCWR. Essentially, these results suggest that on most issues examined (economy, immigration, death penalty, and environment) there is not much difference between the two groups. Differences reside in the focus and themes of their messages on the environment, but particularly on health care, homosexuality, and gender roles, which again may add to the hierarchy's belief that the LCWR was not in line with Church teaching. Yet, their statements do not call for abortion, nor specifically for female ordination, and on homosexuality they do not discuss a change of Church policy but highlight the rigid scope of natural law in terms of human sexuality.

Looking at these organizations' language styles and frames creates an additional layer to examine the claims of the Assessment. Again, it appears that on more issues than not, the nuns and the hierarchy are in agreement and that the LCWR is not mobilizing in areas where they begin to diverge—though their silence, as noted in the Doctrinal Assessment, has been taken as consent to issues of abortion and homosexuality. Yet, as evidenced in the content analyses and interviews, the nuns see a range of social policy issues as pro-life—some of which they have developed an expertise on and are hence empowered to prioritize and advocate. Additionally, the disagreements and even misperceptions that the hierarchy has regarding the LCWR appear to be related to how the social policy issues are framed and to some degree the language style used.

5

On Cue

The Impact of Catholic Religious Elite Messaging on Lay Public Opinion

Thus far I have examined the tension between American Catholic female religious and the hierarchy via an analysis of the Doctrinal Assessment of the LCWR and an exploration of how clergy and nuns work to impact social policy. In doing so, I have argued that the Assessment captures the gendered-leadership dilemma nuns face because it cannot be separated from their institutional position. In this way, the Assessment demonstrates the tension of policy commitments and authority between Catholic female religious and the USCCB. Some of this tension is rooted in the interpretation of Vatican II reforms, which is connected to the sense of policy expertise the nuns have developed over time. The implications are competing principals who deliver competing frames to their publics.

The natural next question is whether these organizations' statements are effective in influencing the laity? Upon immediate exposure to their statements, how do Catholics respond? Which group's messages are more effective in persuading Catholics, the LCWR, or the USCCB? These questions engage the debate about how much religious leaders influence followers' policy preferences. Little of this work has been conducted in the context of the Catholic Church (but see Bjarnasson and Welch 2004 Smith

2008), and, more importantly, none of this work has examined contrasting messages in any religious tradition. Therefore, this analysis can show not just whether Catholic religious leaders can influence the laity but just how far that influence extends. Leadership characteristics (also known more generally as "source cues") are one part of the puzzle of persuasion, and individual dispositions toward the leadership are another. Therefore, I will also assess whether Catholics with a predisposition to authority are more likely to give deference to elite messaging.

Moreover, examining these questions takes the analysis of the Assessment to another level—did the hierarchy have reason to be concerned by the potential influence of the LCWR's statements? Essentially, did the nuns threaten traditional Church authority?

This chapter looks at these remaining questions through an experiment embedded in a survey, analyzing if lay Catholics are influenced by messages on social policy issues by either the USCCB or the LCWR. Experimental approaches are quickly becoming a standard tool in assessing the level and scope of religious elite influence since they allow us to control who is exposed to what message—clearly quite different from voluntarily attending a rally of the Nuns on the Bus tour.

Political Elite Cueing

The work on religious elite cues parallels some of the scholarship on political cue giving, so it is important to first and briefly highlight key findings within this literature. Zaller (1992) argues that elite driven communication has an impact on public opinion and may vary depending on one's level of political awareness. Elite communication can assist citizens in making policy judgments through levels of formal or deductive reasoning (Arnold 1993; Calvert 1985; Lupia and McCubbins 1998; Wittman 1995). Furthermore, the level of effectiveness of elite driven communication may be dependent on citizens' level of like/dislike or trust/distrust regarding the elite source and cue (Kuklinski and Hurley 1994; Mondak 1993a and b; Pomper 1972; Zaller 1992). Political scientists have also looked at how personally knowing the source of a cue is influential. For example, polling data show that Americans have higher levels of trust among local government officials than national leaders (McCarthy 2016). This suggests that a cue coming from a local political elite may be more effective than one from a Washington elite or insider. Knowing the source can act as a simple heuristic, helping the receiver process complex information and make decisions (Arceneaux 2008; Arceneaux and Kolodny 2009; Bartels 2002; Boudreau 2009; Cohen 2003; Druckman 2001a, 2001b; Druckman et al. 2010; Goren, Federico, and Kittilson 2009; Kam 2005; Kuklinski and Hurley 1994; Lau and Redlawsk 2006; Lupia 1994; Nicholson 2011; Rahn 1993).

Religious Elite Cueing

Despite many church's tax-exempt status, clergy remarks and activities can still center on public policy issues. This is important as clergy can and often do work to cue their congregations on various issues (Djupe and Calfano 2012; Djupe and Neiheisel 2008; Guth et al. 1997). Cues can be considered pieces of information that help individuals evaluate positions on a subject without the need to possess an in-depth level of knowledge (Eagly and Chaiken 1993).

American clergy have been found to be heavily involved in politics and well positioned to influence the public. Religious leaders tend to enjoy a level of trust and good standing among members of the faith community and people often seek outside guidance to help make sense of complex social issues (Brady and Sniderman 1985; Djupe and Gilbert 2009; Welch et al. 1993). However, this leadership has focused predominantly on Protestant, male clergy. These scholars have examined the amount, form, and scope of political cue giving by Protestant clergy (Cavendish 2001; Hadden 1969; Jelen 2001; Smidt 2004; Smidt and Schaap 2009; Quinley 1974; Welch et al. 1993). Scholars have also studied how clergy cue giving can vary by religious elites based on levels of resources and opportunity (Crawford and Olson 2001; Guth et al. 1997; Olson 2000).

While most of the work on clergy cues has assumed that they are effective, some find varying and nuanced levels of impact.

For example, Welch et al. (1993) and Crawford and Olson (2001) find that congregants recall hearing sermons on political issues and are receptive to these cues. Yet, Djupe and Gilbert (2009) find that though congregants can recall clergy cues, it does not mean they perceive them correctly. Furthermore, scholars argue that congregants are receptive to political cues by clergy (Djupe and Gilbert 2009; Jelen 2001; Leege, Kellstedt, and Wald 1990) and maybe even more so when these types of cues reflect their preferences (Djupe and Gilbert 2009; Lenski 1966). However, Olson et al. 2003 find that clergy cues on issues pertaining to morality politics, such as calls from pastors to block the adoption of a state lottery, had no impact. Yet, Jelen (2001) also argues that clergy cues are effective when pastors provide biblical claims to support their positions. Using the Notre Dame study data on lay Catholics, Smith (2008) finds limited instances in which clergy had direct effects on the laity. And both Jelen (2003) and Smith (2008) show that priests weigh local pressures with regard to their political action and messaging.

In a time when the field of religion and politics is trying to determine if religious elite communication matters, this leaves Catholic clergy cue giving and influence in need of further exploration. Moreover, there may be differences between how Protestant and Catholic clergy cue give, particularly on political and social issues. For example, priests tend to operate within a different institutional structure than their Protestant counterparts. The American Catholic Church has a more immutable institutional model than Protestant denominations and more regular contact with the laity through the administration of services (Baggett 2006; Byrnes 1993). Therefore, the Catholic Church may be more effective at transmitting a uniform message from the top down compared to other religious denominations (Bjarnason and Welch 2004). Furthermore, due to the universal nature of Catholicism, it being a single-sect faith, and its structure, Catholic priests may not always feel particularly autonomous and thus are more selective about their political behavior and what issues to cue give on. For example, as discussed in Chapter 2 and Kraybill (2016), since the bishops are considered the teaching arm of the Church, they regularly make statements on political issues and disseminate it to the local parish level. As one of the priests stated in Chapter 2, they take their vow to the bishop seriously and look to their direction in terms of what political material to address to the laity. This is somewhat counter to Calfano and Oldmixon (2016) who find that priests tend to rely more on cues from the bishops when it comes to institutional responsibilities rather than their political behavior. Yet, as the monsignor discussed in Chapter 2, the amount of political or social policy cue giving they are able to do can be constrained by the short-notice clergy and parishes are given by the bishop's office in advance of Sunday mass. Additionally, cue giving by Catholic clergy could also vary by region. Bishop Cantu of Las Cruces, a member of the USCCB, explained in his interview that each state also has its own Catholic Conference of Bishops. These councils of bishops discuss regional political issues and disseminate information to dioceses and parishes in their states. Moreover, Holman and Shockley (2017) also discuss how this message filtration and dissemination process can impact the level of clergy cue giving. Other differences on cue giving may be tied to individual priests (and especially the pastor's financial concerns). For instance, Calfano, Oldmixon, and Gray (2014) find that priest cue giving can be influenced by contextual factors and certain reference groups, and, as such, they are sensitive to the prospect of parishioners making financial contribution decisions based on their political behavior.

Notably, the scholarship on cue giving by Catholic female religious and their potential to influence the laity is essentially nonexistent. Again, because Catholic female religious face institutional barriers due to their gender, they cannot advance to clerical positions. As a result, when looking at female religious influence, scholars tend to focus on faiths that permit a female clergy (Djupe and Olson 2013; Olson, Crawford, and Deckman 2005; Deckman et al. 2003; Olson 2000). In this experiment, I expect to find that Catholic religious leaders influence lay public opinion. However, I do expect receiving a message and source from the USCCB will be more effective in influencing Catholic public opinion because they are a recognized authority in the Church.

The experimental study presented here builds on the prior works noted above by examining the immediate and direct effect of religious elite policy messages and/or source cues on Catholic public opinion. This is done without messages being filtered through regional or subordinate levels of clergy and it importantly includes those from Catholic women religious leaders. This is accomplished by showing the effects on Catholic lay opinion from exposure to a message from either the USCCB or the LCWR and whether or not the source cue is known. Therefore, I specifically examine the following treatment groups:

1. Group A: Received USCCB messages with source cues
2. Group B: Received USCCB messages without identifying source cues
3. Group C: Received LCWR messages with source cues
4. Group D: Received LCWR messages without identifying source cues

In doing so, I pay close attention to examining if the effects of a message or source cue vary by the gender of the organizational elites putting out the cue, as well as if the survey respondents' predisposition to authority moderates the impact. This helps answer whether Catholics see female religious leaders as an influential policy authority or if they give deference to bishops. This latter point is important for providing insight into which type of institutional authority is more influential among Catholics—the office or the person. Members of the USCCB have authority rooted in their office, while nuns have to rely on personal authority, a more general type of professional prerogative rooted in service, collective action, and interactions with the laity (Carroll 1981; Brigham 2015).

Experimental Design

Design and Participants

The experiment was programmed in the web-based survey platform Qualtrics; subjects took the survey online and were randomly assigned to one of five groups: a control group or one of four treatment groups noted above.[1] All participants first answered a set of pretreatment questions within the survey that asked various demographic questions. The survey was designed to capture attitudes on four topics: (1) gay rights; (2) women's roles; (3) government aid to the poor; and (4) environmental regulation.[2] Every respondent, whether assigned to the control or one of the treatment groups received the same set of questions on each of the four topics. The order in which the respondents saw the topics and questions was fixed, following the chronology just immediately noted. Furthermore, if a respondent was assigned to a treatment group, they received the consistent group and cue combination throughout answering topics and corresponding questions. So, for example, if a subject was randomly assigned to the Bishops Cue treatment group, they saw the source for the USCCB on all messages across the four topics.

Note that the control group received the pretreatment questions and the same follow-up questions administered to the treatment groups but received no treatment messages or source cues from either religious elite group. As noted above, after taking a pretreatment survey, subjects were randomly assigned to the control group or one of the four treatment groups. For example, the subjects assigned to Group A: Knows USCCB Source Cue would be given a statement from the bishops on homosexuality, followed by several follow-up questions on the issue, and then move on to the next topic (women's roles, followed by government aid to the poor, concluding with environmental regulation). Below is the message from the bishops on homosexuality along with the follow-up questions. Again, this same process would follow for the groups who were given messages from the LCWR.

> Ministry to Persons with a Homosexual Inclination: Guidelines for Pastoral Care November 14, 2006, United States Conference of Catholic Bishops:
>
> The Church recognizes that "marriage exists solely between a man and a woman, who by mutual personal gift, proper and exclusive to themselves, tend toward the com-

> munion of their persons. In this way, they mutually perfect each other, in order to cooperate with God in the procreation and upbringing of new human lives." Consequently, the Church does not support so-called same-sex "marriages" or any semblance thereof, including civil unions that give the appearance of marriage. Church ministers may not bless such unions or promote them in any way, directly or indirectly. Summarily, the Church does not support the adoption of children by same-sex couples since homosexual unions are contrary to the divine plan.

Respondents were presented with the following two questions on a seven-point "strongly support" to "strongly oppose" scale: "To what extent do you support or oppose gay marriage?" and "Do you support or oppose gay or lesbian couples being permitted to adopt children?"

The messages from the USCCB came from pastoral letters and/or official teaching statements via their website. The messages from the LCWR came from their *Resolutions to Action* publication and policy speeches/statements via their website.

As I discuss in further detail in the results section of this chapter, difference of means tests was conducted across the control and treatment groups in order to determine if the dependent variable, Catholic public opinion on the issue examined, varied depending on which group respondents were in, which tells us whether there was an immediate effect and whether knowing the source of the message caused any significant shift.

Regarding, the survey subjects, just over one thousand self-identified Catholics in the United States were randomly selected to participate in this experiment from the online panel administered by Survey Sample International, which is a premier provider of sampling, data collection, analytic solutions, and tools for survey research. Survey Sample International has the operational capacity to compile a variety of randomized and specified samples to suit researcher's needs, hence the reason for the selection of this firm for this project (www.surveysampling.com). In order to get a sense of this sample, summary statistics and balancing tests were per-

TABLE 5.1. DEMOGRAPHIC COMPARISON OF SURVEY SAMPLE TO NATIONAL DATA ON CATHOLICS		
Demographic Variables	Experimental Survey	National Averages
Age	29% (25–35 years old) 17% (36–45 years old)	41% (30–49 years old)
Gender	37% (Male) 63% (Female)	46% (Male) 54% (Female)
Race/Ethnicity	48% (White) 41.2% (Hispanic) 4.1% (Black) 5.7% (Asian) 1% (Other)	58% (White) 30% (Hispanic) 3% (Black) 5% (Asian) 4% (Other)
U.S. Born	87%	76%
Married	51%	53%
Income	21% ($50,000–$74,999)	22% ($50,000–$74,999)
Party ID	23% (Republican) 48% (Democrat) 24% (Independent) 5% (Something else)	37% (Republican) 41% (Democrat) 22% (Independents)
Education	30% (College grad)	24% (College grad)
Mass Attendance	19% (Weekly) 19% (Almost weekly)	41% (Weekly)

formed before further analysis. The balancing tests showed that the demographic variables were balanced across the treatment and control groups.[3] The summary statistics showed that most of the sample ranged in their early to midthirties, were female (63 percent), were fairly split between identifying as white (48 percent) and Hispanic (41.2 percent), were born in the United States (87 percent), were associated themselves mostly with the Democratic Party (48 percent), and had at least some college education (30 percent). The sample also found more than half to be practicing their faith, in that more than half of the respondents reported regularly attending mass: with those attending weekly comprising (19 percent), those going almost every week making up (19 percent), and up to once a month (16 percent). Table 5.1 compares the demographic variables of my sample to Catholics on a national level.[4]

Overall, the two yield notable similarities in terms of the age range, marital status, income, and education level. For areas such as party identification, my sample showed the same pattern of Catholics identifying more with the Democratic Party, more U.S. born than not, and an ethnic majority of white over other racial/ethnic groups with Hispanics as the second largest group. The only distinction between the two is that my sample comprises a higher level of females than the national average (by 9 points) and a higher level of Hispanics (by 11.2 points).

Hypotheses

Due to mixed findings in support of the theory that religious elites have the ability to influence public opinion, there are areas in need of further exploration. This chapter begins to extend the current theories on the religious elite's influence by examining the impact of receiving a message and/or source cue from a male religious or female religious leadership group of the same faith. Do these elements cause a significant shift of Catholic opinion in the direction of those organizations' social policy positions? Furthermore, since I am interested in the tension of policy and authority between the bishops and nuns, it is important to ask if Catholics with a predisposition to authority are more likely to be influenced by the male-dominated USCCB or female-dominated LCWR. Therefore, the following hypotheses are proffered:

H1: Receiving a message from religious elites causes a shift in Catholic public opinion, particularly when the source cue is known.

H2: Receiving a message from the USCCB and knowing the source cue will be more effective in moving Catholic public opinion than receiving a message from the LCWR and knowing the source cue.

H3: Catholics with a predisposition to the authority will give greater deference to the messages from the USCCB rather than from the LCWR.

Before moving on to the first part of the analysis covering the difference of means across treatment groups, I would like to give some additional attention for the explanation of the third hypothesis. I expect to find that Catholics with a predisposition to authority will be more influenced by the USCCB's message and source cues than the LCWR's. Scholars argue that authoritarianism is a socially learned, stable condition, involving a clustering of attitudes, feelings of submission, opposition to nonconformists, and concern with the proper balance between group authority and individual autonomy (Altemeyer 1981, 1988, and 1996; Stenner 2005). I have chosen to conclude the findings of this chapter with an analysis examining predisposition of authority and support for female priests, same-sex marriage, and gay adoption opinions, because they are more specifically related to the charges discussed in the Assessment of radical feminism and the LCWR's lack of promoting Church teaching on homosexuality (Vatican 2012). This claim signals that the LCWR's stance shows a lack of deference to authority of the Church on this issue.

Overall, I argue that Catholics with a predisposition to authority will give deference to the bishops on the issue of female ordination, same-sex marriage, and gay adoption, particularly those who are exposed to the USCCB source cue. As discussed in the interviews in Chapter 2, Catholics have been culturally groomed to associate authority more readily with the male clergy, even when female religious are in parish leadership positions, such as pastoral coordinator. This parallels literature on male versus female authority that demonstrates leadership has traditionally been assessed using male norms and, therefore, stereotypes frame men as a more natural fit for leadership positions (Eagly and Karau 1992; Chliwniak 1997; Heilman 2001). This is no different for institutions of faith, which overwhelmingly have been associated with male authority (Watling 2002). Moreover, according to a PEW Research Center report, even in faiths that permit female clergy there is a lack of women religious in top leadership and administrative positions, which is even more pronounced in the Catholic Church, which strongly opposes female ordination to the priesthood (Sandstrom 2016). Therefore, the argument can be made that male religious authority has a premium and prominence over female religious authority, particularly for those in the faith predisposed to this characteristic.

Results

Part I: Difference of Means across Treatment Groups

In order to determine how the opinions of each treatment group varied across conditions, difference of means tests were conducted. Overall, the results suggest that receiving a message from a religious elite group (such as the USCCB or LCWR) influenced the positions of those in the treatment groups—their opinions tended to differ from those in the control group, demonstrating an immediate effect. However, knowing the source cue appears to have mixed results; the USCCB cue overall yielded more significant results than the LCWR cue.

Homosexuality

The questions on gay marriage and adoption were posed on a seven-point scale with lower values indicating more progressive positions and higher ones indicating more conservative stances. The statement from the USCCB on this issue advocated its position against both same-sex marriage and gay adoption. The statement from the LCWR demonstrated it is more inclusive and accepting of homosexuality in the Church (see Appendix for the full listing of statements and follow-up questions).

As figure 5.1 shows, the mean of the control group on both issues, of gay marriage and adoption, indicates that respondents lean toward neither support nor opposition. These results are not necessarily in line with the more conservative position of the USCCB. Regarding the treatment groups, both the Bishops Cue and Bishops No Cue group yielded the most significant treatment effects on these questions. The respondents in the Bishops treatment groups moved in the direction of the USCCB's more traditional position of

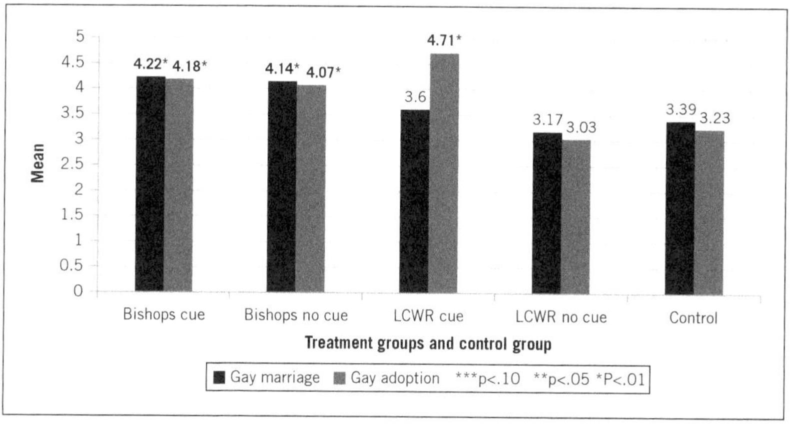

Figure 5.1. Treatment effects on gay rights attitudes (difference of means test).

opposition to same-sex marriage and gay adoption. Overall, there is a negligible difference between the Bishops Cue and Bishops No Cue group on these questions, perhaps indicating that the message is more effective than the source cue.

Regarding the LCWR treatment groups, their difference of means scores suggest movement toward greater support for same-sex marriage, but the results are not significant. This is interesting since the nuns have a more progressive position on this issue, one might expect that exposure to the LCWR's message and/or cue would move participants in a more accepting direction of same-sex marriage. Regarding the issue of gay adoption, the results show that those in the LCWR Cue treatment group reject the cue.

Women's Role in Society and the Church

Several of the questions examined Catholic public opinion on women's role in society and the Church. These questions focused on whether women should have an equal role with men in running business, industry, and government, whether or not women's contributions are respected equally to men's in the Catholic Church, and, last, if women should be permitted in the priesthood. Overall, the bishops have a more traditional position on gender roles that is rooted in natural law while the nuns have a more egalitarian

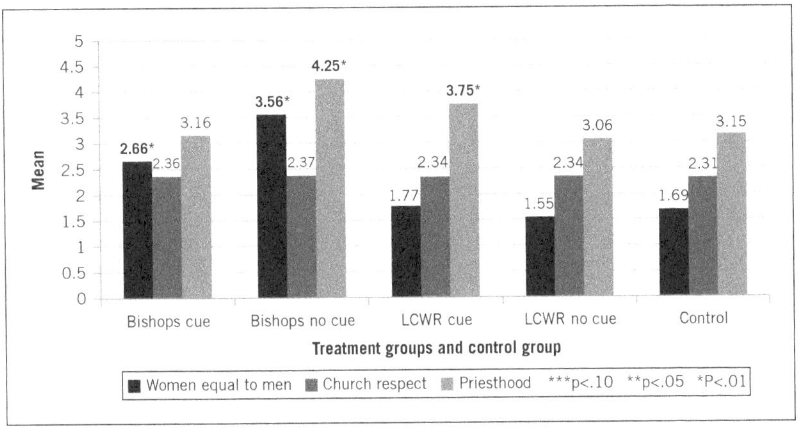

Figure 5.2. Treatment effects on women's role attitudes (difference of means test).

view of gender roles that calls for more empowerment of women in the Church. The results of the difference of means test are shown in figure 5.2.

The first question regarding women's role in society was posed on a seven-point scale, with lower values suggesting that women should have an equal role to men and higher mean values signaling a move toward more traditional and conservative positions. The results for the control group demonstrate that respondents tended to believe that women should have an equal role in society. The results for the LCWR Cue and LCWR No Cue treatment groups also indicated that respondents maintained the same attitude as the control, that women should have an equal role in society.

In line with expectations, those in both of the USCCB treatment groups were significantly less likely to support women having an equal role in society. Particularly, respondents in the Bishops No Cue group indicated higher mean scores with them leaning more toward women not having an equal role. In fact, those who received the USCCB cue express more egalitarian attitudes than the no cue group, though still less egalitarian than the control.

The next question was designed to capture whether the respondents felt that the Catholic Church respected the contributions of men or women more. This question was coded on a three-point scale: (1) the Church respects the contributions of women more than it respects the contributions of men; (2) the Church respects the contributions of both men and women equally; and (3) the Church respect the contributions of men more than it respects the contributions of women. None of the results across the groups on this particular question were significant, and they indicated that among the control and treatment groups, most of the respondents felt that contributions were respected equally. Interestingly, respondents in the LCWR Cue and LCWR No Cue groups did not indicate feeling that men were more respected then women, as they moved in the direction of feeling that the Church respects the roles of men and women equally. This is unexpected since some of the LCWR's statements indicate a position of women not receiving the same level of respect as men in the Church, so here the LCWR cue and message are not necessarily accepted.

Last, the question of whether women should be permitted in the priesthood yielded some surprising results. This question was posed on a seven-point scale with lower values indicating more agreement in accepting females into the priesthood (leaning more toward the position of the LCWR) and higher values indicating disagreement (moving more toward the position of the USCCB). Again, it is important to note that the USCCB holds to the official Church position of not permitting female ordination and that the LCWR is more supportive of women being able to take on full participation within the faith. The mean score of the control group indicated that respondents lean toward agreeing that females should be permitted in the priesthood. The results show that the Bishops No Cue treatment group moved significantly in the direction of not agreeing with permitting females in the priesthood while the Bishops Cue group showed no effect. Whatever the reason, Catholics are responding negatively to the Bishops, though showing that they could affirm the substance of their message. Moreover, curiously, those in the LCWR Cue group also demonstrated a more conservative position, rejecting the cue. This again is also interesting as one may have anticipated that those who heard from the LCWR on this issue would be more supportive of women in the priesthood. Respondents may discount the LCWR as a source of authority in the Church, or may have heard of the Doctrinal Assessment and view the group as a counter to official Church teaching. Either way, they are not moving in the LCWR's direction.

Government Aid to the Poor

Several questions were also asked in order to determine if Catholic public opinion on government aid to the poor was affected by receiving messages and cues from either the USCCB or the LCWR. The questions posed to respondents dealt with whether government spending on the poor should be (1) increased, (2) stay the same, (3) decreased, or (4) cut out entirely. The other question asked respondents if it was the responsibility of the government to ensure people had a job and a good standard of living. Once again, higher mean scores indicate the more conservative position of not favoring more money in the federal budget for assistance and more individual responsibility in getting ahead economically. As previously mentioned, assisting the poor is a major component of Catholicism, which both the USCCB and LCWR address and advocate in their policy promulgations. Both organizations refer to the federal budget as a "moral" document and the need for the government to assist vulnerable populations, such as the poor (Clark 2011; USCCB 2012c). This is a case where both organizations have similar positions; therefore, mean scores of lower values would indicate Catholic public opinion moving in both of these organizations' directions, essentially aligning with the Church on this issue.

The results for this topic are captured in figure 5.3, which show strong existing support for aid to the poor. The results indicate that respondents in the treatment group that know the source cue and receive a message from the USCCB were significantly affected and moved away from increasing government spending on the poor and toward keeping it the same. Interestingly, those receiving the same message from the USCCB but without the source cue had similar effects of the control group, indicating spending levels on the poor should stay near the same. This was also the case in both treatment groups receiving messages from the LCWR; however,

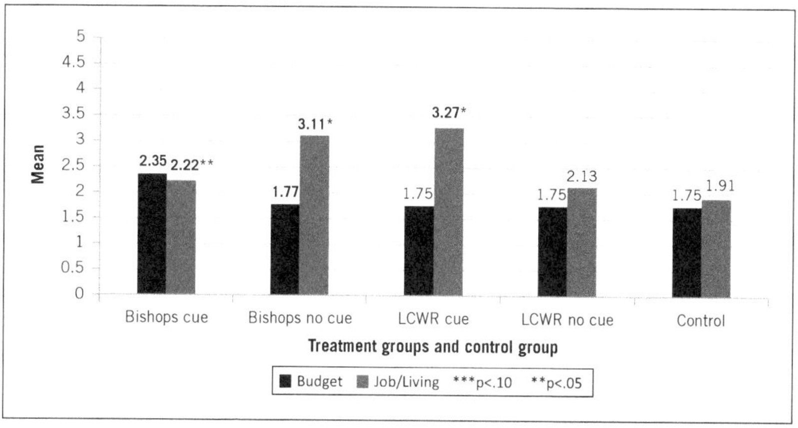

Figure 5.3. Treatment effects on government aid to the poor attitudes (difference of means test).

results from these three remaining groups did not yield significant effects. Overall, Catholics in the Bishops Cue group rejected the cue from the bishops since their results yielded significantly higher mean scores on the issue of the budget (meaning a more conservative position on aid to the poor) than the other treatment groups and control group. The control and remaining treatment (LCWR Cue and LCWR No Cue) scores were not significant but indicated greater support for government assistance to the poor than the USCCB source cue group.

Figure 5.3 also captures the difference of means across the control and treatment groups on how respondents felt about the government's responsibility to ensure each person has a job and good standard of living or whether individuals should be responsible for their own employment and standard of living. Respondents in the control group showed a tendency to believe that it is the government's responsibility to ensure a good standard of living and occupation, which is aligned with Catholic social teaching on this issue. The LCWR Cue was rejected, and this was significant, as was the message from the Bishops No Cue Group. Compared to the control group, the Bishop's Cue group had a significant and slightly higher mean score (though not as high as the No Bishops Cue or LCWR Cue groups).

Environment

Finally, respondents were asked about current regulations to protect the environment. In a similar fashion to the topic of government assistance to the poor, both of these organizations advocate more environmental regulation to protect vulnerable populations from pollution and climate change. The LCWR tends to address the threats posed to women as a result of environmental degradation more so than the USCCB. The difference of means results is captured in figure 5.4. While the results differ significantly from the control, the effects are in the opposite direction from what is expected. Catholics in the treatment groups, without variation, show more conservative attitudes on environmental regulations, which indicates that Catholics are not accepting the message or cues of either religious elite group.

The second question posed on the environment asked respondents on a seven-point scale to what extent they felt the environment was a feminist issue. Lower scores indicated that they agreed, and higher mean values indicated that they disagreed. As discussed above, the USCCB does not view threats to the environment as a feminist issue, but the LCWR does. Respondents in the control group demonstrated a position of neither agreeing nor disagreeing, as was essentially the same across treatment groups with none of the results yielding any significant differences. The third question posed on the environment asked whether respondents agreed or disagreed on a seven-point scale that they had a spiritual obligation to the environment. Again, lower scores indicated that they agreed, and higher mean values indicated that they disagreed. Both the USCCB and the LCWR discuss individuals as serving as stewards of the environment and discuss a religious and moral obligation to take care of it. The results are fairly similar across the control and treatment groups, which indicate that respondents "agreed" to "somewhat agreed" that they had a spiritual obligation to be responsible stewards of the environment; however, none of these results were significant. This indicates that opinions across the groups were already consistent and the treatments had a negligible, if any, impact. Last, the respondents were asked to rank on a similar seven-point scale if they agreed or disagreed that climate

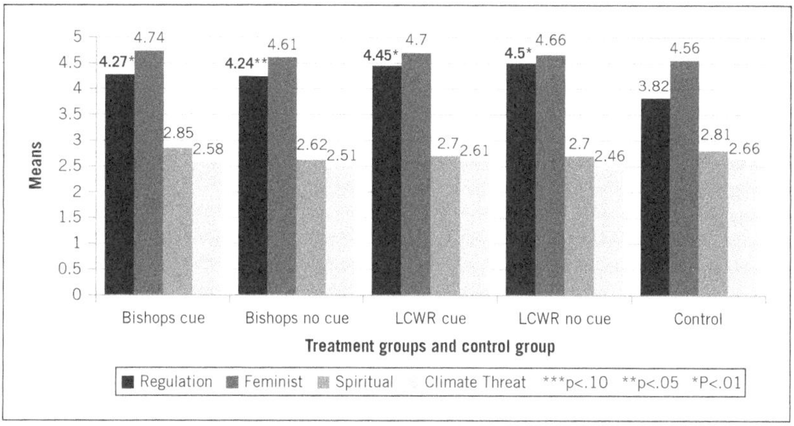

Figure 5.4. Treatment effects on environmental regulation attitudes (difference of means test).

change posed a serious threat to people around the world. As is the case with the previous topic, this is a question/issue on which both the USCCB and LCWR maintain a similar position that climate change poses a threat to both the environment and people. The results are fairly similar across the control and treatment groups, indicating that respondents "agreed" to "somewhat agreed" that climate change poses a threat to people around the world; however, none of these results were significant. Opinions across the groups were already consistent, and the treatments did not have much of an effect.

Part II: Predisposition to Authority

Since so much of the USCCB's response to the LCWR pivoted on who holds proper authority in the Church, I sought to assess if Catholics with a predisposition to authority were more likely to be influenced by the USCCB or the LCWR. The focus here is on two topics: support for women in the priesthood and homosexuality (via questions on same-sex marriage and gay adoption). The Assessment specifically expressed concerns the Church had regarding the LCWR's positions on these issues, and the treatment messages used in this experiment by the bishops and nuns addressed these topics, providing an opportunity to directly test how Catholics with a predisposition to authority would respond.

Predisposition to authority was separately interacted with each of the control and treatment groups in a regression model. Predisposition to authority has been measured by asking respondents to choose which word appeals the most to them in a pair, such as "obey or question," "rules or progress," "obedience or curiosity," along with questions on which characteristic is more important for a child to have, "a child obeys his parents vs. a child is responsible for his or her own actions," "a child has respect for his elders vs. a child thinks for him or herself" (Hetherington and Weiler 2005; Merolla and Zechmeister 2009; Stenner 2005). If respondents answered in the direction of authority, it was coded "1" and, if not, it was coded "0." For example, "obey" was coded 1 and "question" coded 0. I used a factor analysis to group the questions into similar dimensions and identify latent variables (Rahn 2016). The variables loaded best on to one factor, which I use in this analysis, labeled auth1 (note on result tables this is listed as "Authority"), which had the highest variance of 1.94 (and an eigenvalue of 2.28) and, therefore, it was used to interact with the control and each of the treatment group conditions. Support for women in the priesthood, same-sex marriage, and gay adoption were coded on a seven-point scale with lower values indicating more progressive positions and higher ones indicating more conservative stances. I first discuss the results of predisposition to authority and support for women priests, then move on to the impact of this characteristic on Catholic support for same-sex marriage and gay adoption across the control and treatment groups.

Women Priests

The results in table 5.2 show the effect of predisposition of authority on Catholic opinion toward women in the priesthood.[5] When looking at the first column capturing the isolated variable representing predisposition to authority, we see Catholics with this predisposition are significantly moving in the direction of not supporting women priests.[6] When moving to the next column and looking at each isolated group, Catholics in the control

TABLE 5.2. SUPPORT FOR WOMEN PRIESTS, MODERATING EFFECTS ACROSS CONTROL AND TREATMENT GROUPS			
	Authority	Group	Group * Authority
Control:	-.2296*	-.3986*	-.0669
	(.0676)	(.1440)	(.1452)
Bishops Cue:	-.2346*	-.3672**	-.0547
	(.0671)	(.1495)	(.1487)
Bishops No Cue:	-.3575*	.9563*	.5360*
	(.0649)	(.1464)	(.1495)
LCWR Cue:	-.1945*	.3282**	-.3181**
	(.0654)	(.1583)	(.1614)
LCWR No Cue:	-.2461*	-.5518*	-.0531
	(.0671)	(.1494)	(.1469)

Adjust R-squared
Control: 0.0208
Bishops Cue: 0.0191
Bishops No Cue: 0.0653
LCWR Cue: 0.0209
LCWR No Cue: 0.0261
***$p<0.10$, **$p<.05$, *$p<.01$

(p=.006), Bishops Cue (p=.014), and LCWR No Cue (p=.000) are also significantly moving in the direction of not supporting women priests. Here, it is the No Bishops Cue/message (p=.000) that is rejected and the LCWR Cue (p=.038) which is accepted, as respondents in both groups are significantly moving in the direction of supporting female ordination. Finally, in looking at the third column of the table, Catholics with a predisposition to authority in the control and Bishops Cue groups are moving in the direction the Church in not supporting women priests, but the results are not significant. Furthermore, the bishops' message is rejected, as those with a predisposition to authority in the No Bishops Cue group are moving in the direction of supporting women priests and the results are significant (p=.000). Overall, when looking at the variable just representing predisposition to authority, Catholics possessing this characteristic do not support the idea of women priests; however, as the interacted effects show, that does not necessarily translate over to them accepting the bishops' authority/message on this issue. Notably, the interactions also show that those with a predisposition to authority do not accept the nuns as an authority on this issue, rejecting both the cue and message and moving in the direction of not supporting women in the priesthood. This was particularly significant for those possessing this characteristic in the LCWR Cue group (p=.049).

Homosexuality

In looking at support for same-sex marriage, the results in table 5.3 show once again that Catholics with a predisposition to authority are significantly moving in the direction of not supporting gay rights on this issue. However, turning attention to the second column, respondents in the control and treatment groups demonstrate mixed findings. Here we see that Catholics in the control group do not support same-sex marriage and the results are significant (p=.036). In comparison, the Bishops and No Bishops Cue groups show that Catholics are rejecting both the clergy's cue and message, significantly moving in the direction of supporting same-sex marriage (both p=.000). Furthermore, both the nuns' cue and message are also rejected, with respondents moving in the direction of not supporting same-sex marriage, with the LCWR No Cue treatment group yielding significant effects (p=.000). In looking at the third column of the table, showcasing the interacted effects, we see in comparison to the control group that Catholics with a predisposition to authority and in the Bishops Cue and No Bishops Cue treatments groups reject both the bishops' cue and message, moving in the direction of supporting same-sex marriage, though neither of the results are significant. However, Catholics with this characteristic in the LCWR No Cue treatment group appear to accept the nuns' message, but the results here too are not significant. Once again, the findings suggest that Catholics with a predisposition to authority may have traditional positions on social issues, but that does not necessarily mean they are impacted by Church authority. And, again, the results show that the nuns are not clear opinion leaders either.

Finally, in turning our attention to table 5.4, we observe yet again that Catholics with a predisposition to authority are signifi-

TABLE 5.3. SUPPORT FOR SAME-SEX MARRIAGE, MODERATING EFFECTS ACROSS CONTROL AND TREATMENT GROUPS

	Authority	Group	Group * Authority
Control:	-.4667*	-.3275**	-.0647
	(.0771)	(.1559)	(.1569)
Bishops Cue:	-.5174*	.6773*	.1774
	(.0728)	(.1815)	(.1822)
Bishops No Cue:	-.4993*	.6029*	.05653
	(.0742)	(.1706)	(.1708)
LCWR Cue:	-.4536*	-.0644	-.2111
	(.0732)	(.1823)	(.1849)
LCWR No Cue:	-.5159*	-.6859*	.0738
	(.0761)	(.1600)	(.1579)

Adjust R-squared
Control: 0.0582
Bishops Cue: 0.0685
Bishops No Cue: 0.0632
LCWR Cue: 0.0550
LCWR No Cue: 0.0725
***$p<0.10$, **$p<.05$, *$p<.01$

cantly moving in the direction of not supporting gay adoption. In focusing on the control and treatment groups in the second column, the results show that Catholics in the Bishops Cue, No Bishops Cue, and LCWR Cue treatment groups are significantly affected, moving in the direction of supporting gay rights on this issue (p=.002; p=.008; p=.000, respectively). The findings also show that the message of the nuns' is rejected, demonstrating here that the cue was more impactful. In looking at the final column of the table, capturing the interacted effects, the results are mixed. For example, the findings show that Catholics in the control group with a predisposition to authority do not support gay adoption and the results are significant (p=.113). This is a similar result to Catholics possessing this characteristic in the No Bishops Cue group, but the results are not significant. However, Catholics with a predisposition to authority in the Bishops Cue group reject the cue, moving in the direction of supporting gay adoption, although

TABLE 5.4. SUPPORT FOR GAY ADOPTION, MODERATING EFFECTS ACROSS CONTROL AND TREATMENT GROUP			
	Authority	Group	Group * Authority
Control:	-.2431**	-.6231*	-.2578***
	(.0834)	(.1618)	(.1625)
Bishops Cue:	-.3572*	.5914*	.2387
	(.0791)	(.1928)	(.1928)
Bishops No Cue:	-.2791*	.4801*	-.1602
	(.0802)	(.1812)	(.1820)
LCWR Cue:	-.4096*	1.091*	.6927*
	(.0744)	(.2249)	(.2445)
LCWR No Cue:	-.2783*	-.9461*	-.2398
	(.0821)	(.1665)	(.1642)

Adjust *R*-squared
Control: 0.0372
Bishops Source: 0.0304
Bishops No Source: 0.0260
LCWR Source: 0.0624
LCWR No Source: 0.0543
***$p<0.10$, **$p<.05$, *$p<.01$

the results are not significant. When looking at Catholics with a predisposition to authority in the LCWR Cue group, the nuns' cue is accepted, with respondents significantly moving in the direction of supporting gay adoption ($p=.005$); however, when the source cue is not known, respondents reject the message from the LCWR, though the results are not significant. Again, a pattern emerges where Catholics with a predisposition to authority demonstrate socially conservative/traditional positions, but that does not mean they are consistently influenced by Church authority/religious leaders.

Discussion and Implications

These findings demonstrate receiving a message from religious elites can have an immediate effect on Catholic public opinion, evidenced by the shifts from the control group. However, as the results show, for some the message is more important and for others knowing the source is critical. In the first part of the analysis, the difference of means tests results show that more messages and cues were accepted from the USCCB than the LCWR. This may be the result of a couple of factors. First, Catholics are perhaps more familiar with the USCCB and are therefore exposed to their messages more often than the LCWR. For example, Lupia (1994) argues that familiarity can influence the level of impact that a source cue has.

Furthermore, more rejection of the LCWR cues and messages may also stem from the Doctrinal Assessment given to the LCWR by the Church. The Assessment spurred support, but perhaps not necessarily among all Catholics. So respondents may see the LCWR as illegitimate or insubordinate and reject its cues and messages. Rejection of the LCWR source cue may also stem from a lack of clarity among respondents on what is meant by the organization's title, "The Leadership Conference of Women Religious." Perhaps respondents were not clear on what was meant by the terms "leadership" or "women religious." Respondents might have been clearer and understanding if the cue specified that they were nuns, just as the USCCB cue specifies they are bishops, which most Catholics know as members of the clergy.

Again, the results from the difference of means tests show that the messages and cues from the USCCB are more effective than those from the LCWR. The difference of means tests show that the LCWR cues and messages supporting female priests as well as gay marriage and adoption were rejected by respondents. The same occurred with respect to the LCWR's position on the government's responsibility to ensure an equal standard of living for people.

In looking at the second part of the analysis, focusing on the moderating effects of Catholics with a predisposition to authority, we see interesting results. First, in just looking at those predisposed to authority, outside of the moderating effects, the findings show that Catholics possessing this characteristic hold more traditional positions, being less likely to support women priests, same-sex marriage, and gay adoption. When turning attention to the moderating effects, we see more varied results, suggesting that having a predisposition to authority may not necessarily translate over to these Catholics accepting Church authority. For Catholics predisposed to authority not only are the bishops not a consistent authority/influence but neither is the LCWR. Importantly, both the difference of means tests and the results from the moderating effects show that the nuns are not seen as a consistent authority figure in the Church. These findings call into question the hierarchy's level of scrutiny toward the LCWR in the Assessment and the concern that nuns threatened the bishops' authority in the American Catholic Church.

6

Male Clergy and Female Religious

A Concluding Note on Living the Faith from Two Types of Authority

On the morning of April 16, 2015, news headlines across the country read, "Vatican Ends Battle with U.S. Catholic Nuns' Group" (Goodstein 2015) and "Vatican Ends Controversial Three-Year Oversight of U.S Sisters' Leaders" (McElwee 2015). The CDF announced that they had accepted a joint report from the LCWR and the American bishops overseeing the mandate and organization's renewal. In a statement discussing the end of the renewal, the LCWR maintained that from the start of the process they had "serious concerns" about the Assessment and "believed that the sanctions called for by the CDF were disproportionate to the concerns raised" (LCWR 2015).

The Assessment reveals a story of tension between the nuns and the hierarchy that some argue was decades in the making (Neuman 2012). At the core of this story is the gendered nature of authority in the Church, which is related to the tension between both groups' policy positions and expertise. For the bishops, authority is rooted in the institutional Church and hence their office (Carroll 1981; *Catechism of the Catholic Church* 2010). The nuns have a sense of personal authority derived from their experience as women religious working closely with the laity, their high levels of education and professionalism, and importantly their interpretation of key Vatican II reforms. Thus, the Assessment put on display two competing authorities within the American Catholic Church. It seems the hierarchy was aware of this dynamic and that the Assessment's accusatory and aggressive tone was in part an effort to silence the sisters and remind them of their place within the Church. Religious institutions have long regarded women as a silent class of membership, and religious authority has been more associated with men, tasking them as the creators and guardians of doctrine, as well as the developers of institutional rules, policies, and positions (Watling 2002). Women have challenged this paradigm and made gains in other religious traditions; however, females occupying top faith leadership positions are still limited (Sandstrom 2016).

The purpose of this book has been to examine this tension that arises over issues of policy and authority between female religious and male clergy in the American Catholic Church. I have done so by examining how the hierarchy felt threatened by the use of the nuns' personal authority on social policy issues, as showcased in the charges of the Doctrinal Assessment. The findings demonstrate that the nuns were not taking positions counter to the Church per se but instead prioritizing, framing, and employing different language in their social policy messages. These competing elements gave way to tension between the LCWR and the hierarchy. This study has also captured how the nuns have learned to navigate this tension by strategically choosing when to collaborate with the hierarchy to advance common social policy objectives, as evidenced by their working on USCCB committees, attending their staff working group meetings, and coordinating lobbying efforts on Capitol Hill. I also raised the question of whether either the USCCB or the LCWR have influence over the policy preferences of Catholics, finding that the bishops' messages are overall more effective. However, when focusing on Catholics with a predisposition to authority, the results are more mixed, showing that those with this characteristic may hold a more traditional position on the social issues considered, but when presented with a cue or message from the bishops (the teaching authority in the American Catholic

Church), they are not necessarily impacted. Essentially suggesting that having a predisposition to authority does not necessarily mean Catholics accept Church authority.

Essentially, the Assessment generated a valuable opportunity to compare the influence of Catholic male and female religious leaders in their work to influence social policy and the laity. Little prior scholarship has looked this in depth at Catholic female religious' policy influence and instead has concentrated more on Churches that permit female clergy (i.e., select Protestant denominations). Furthermore, no previous work to date has directly examined the claims of the Doctrinal Assessment via an examination of the statements on which the nuns were accused of being outside of Church teaching. Few studies have compared policy statements of male and female religious leaders of the same faith in order to see how and if they differ in terms of priorities, positions, framing, and language style. Therefore, to my knowledge, this is the only study that has sought to systematically analyze the CDF's claims by examining the actual policy statements of the LCWR. By comparing them to the USCCB, we learned that the LCWR had valid reason to claim that the Assessment was flawed and not reflective of their "lived experience" (Bauman 2013).

Some of the disagreement between these groups appears to be rooted in their priority and framing of a few critical social policy issues: health care, homosexuality, and gender equality. However, the nuns did not take positions counter to the Church per se on these three topics. For example, the findings of this study show that the LCWR did not advocate for abortion, nor endorse same-sex marriage, nor call directly for female ordination. Instead, on abortion the nuns simply did not address the issue and focused on what they felt were other pro-life concerns. Consequentially, the nuns did endorse the ACA of 2010; at the time, the bishops opposed the ACA due to their concerns it would federally fund abortion. As the interviews in Chapter 2 highlight, the nuns felt the legislation had enough protections regarding the Church's pro-life stance. Additionally, due to their experience as female religious working with women, children, and other vulnerable populations who are intimately impacted by access to health care, the LCWR decided to become signers on a letter issued to Congress expressing support for the bill. For the nuns this was a prolife position. These women religious were essentially flexing their personal authority and drawing on their own policy experience within the field of health care in taking this position. For some, this showing of authority appeared to challenge the institutional Church's stance via the USCCB.

A similar dynamic is at play with issues surrounding female ordination and homosexuality. Once again, an analysis of the documents indicates that the nuns do not advocate for same-sex marriage but rather call for full inclusion and acceptance of gay Catholics. It is important to note that the LCWR does not call for any mobilization activity on these issues. In regard to female ordination, the documents show that the LCWR does not call for women to become priests but rather calls for an increased role in decision making. Therefore, when the Assessment claims that the LCWR had policy positions of "corporate dissent" pertaining to issues of homosexuality and female ordination, the analysis here shows otherwise. Yes, the nuns have a more inclusive and empowered position on these issues, but they are not taking stances in clear opposition to the Church's positions. It appears that the Church felt their authority was threatened by the LCWR's mere inclusive advocacy on these issues.

Furthermore, it also appears that the hierarchy misunderstood the LCWR's silence on homosexuality as outright consent. Here, a few things are at play. First, again, the LCWR never specifically states a position on homosexuality that is counter to teaching (e.g., promoting same-sex marriage); instead they call for compassion and for the faith to ensure a home for gay people within the Church (Zollman 2003). And, second, women religious, like those in the LCWR, who are again traditionally seen as the silent, cooperative, and complementary partners in institutions of faith (Watling 2002), are in this case being criticized and scrutinized for their expected role. In the end, this gave the Church the perception that the LCWR was not toeing a harsh enough line on these issues and hence was not comporting with institutional authority. However, if the institutional Church's role is more focused on dogma and doctrine, or as Sister Simone Campbell states "doing the rules," then the nuns are not acting out of turn here by exercising their personal authority and vocation. Instead, Sister Simone Campbell says their job is "to take the Gospel to where it wouldn't be otherwise. And the freedom as a women religious is that I am not caught in the clerical hierarchical structure." This is most likely where the nuns felt like the accusations and sanctions called for in the Assessment "were disproportionate to the concerns raised" (LCWR 2015). This also shows that some of the tension over authority is in part due to their different roles: religious versus clerical life. It appears that the bishops and the hierarchy can get very focused on the institutional aspects of the faith and do not always have an understanding of the religious life of the Church—meaning those working outside of the hierarchical model. As the LCWR explained in a *New York Times* interview one month after the conclusion of the Assessment, they had to explain these differences to the delegate bishops overseeing the renewal, noting that a "breakthrough" finally occurred in the last month of the process when they met with Pope Francis, a Jesuit, who comes from a background of religious life (Goodstein 2015).

Through an examination of the LCWR and USCCB's policy statements, along with the interviews conducted with nuns and members of the clergy, we see that both male and female religious work to influence social policy and lay Catholic public opinion. We also see that in doing so, male and female religious leaders within the Church take different approaches. These approaches cannot be separated from the gendered-institutional design of the Church; as female religious must navigate the boundaries of the faith differently than their male clerical counterparts.

For example, the nuns have also learned that sometimes it works to the benefit of their policy objectives to exercise personal authority as opposed to partnering with institutional authority. Though they fell under much scrutiny, it worked to the nuns' benefit in terms of achieving policy goals to act on personal authority and endorse the ACA. In the end, the nuns were a key factor in getting the legislation passed, as directly noted in a speech by President Barack Obama at the 2015 Catholic Health Association Conference (Jenkins 2017; Kraybill 2017; Reed 2015). Interestingly, in the current debate on whether to repeal and replace the ACA under the Trump administration and Republican-controlled Congress, the USCCB has done "an about face," and rallied to support the ACA. For example, on January 18, 2017, the USCCB, paralleling the nuns' tactic in 2010, issued its own letter to Congress expressing concerns about the repeal efforts and urging members to preserve health care coverage. I would argue (though the bishops may not admit it or agree) that the nuns' efforts demonstrated that supporting the ACA was in fact an effective pro-life decision, as it resulted in millions more Americans being insured and thousands receiving life-saving care (Hiltzik 2017; Bakalar 2017). Overall, this is an example of female religious exercising their personal authority and, in doing so, serving as leadership models on public policy for the Church.

Though female religious have been influential in terms of impacting social policy, we learn through the experimental analysis of Chapter 5 that lay Catholics are not consistently influenced by their advocacy, nor do they see them as a recognized authority. As previously discussed, the Catholic Church is a gendered institution and as such has not yet meaningfully instilled a culture of respect for female leadership. This was evidenced in Chapter 2 when the female religious and lay women in administrative positions such as pastoral coordinator discussed how their credentials are questioned by the laity.

The results do show that messages from religious leaders can have an immediate effect—treatment groups who received statements from the nuns and bishops had distinguishable reactions from the unprompted control group. However, the findings were mixed across topics, importantly indicating that the Church struggles to be a consistent authority among Catholics across social policy topics. This may be a result of the Church straddling both liberal and conservative positions and relaying them to a laity that is also not uniformly political. This is a challenge for the bishops in American politics. For example, the findings show that on certain issues, such as gay rights, the bishops' cues and messages tend to be more effective than on issues pertaining to government aid to the poor.

The results of the experiment demonstrate several key factors. First, that authority has been culturally defined as male leadership rather than female leadership in the Church as the findings show more deference was given to the bishops than the nuns on the issues considered. This is particularly interesting in light of some data showing Catholic support for female ordination (Burge 2017; Sandstrom 2016). It may be in the case that when the bishops are deferred to it is because respondents are more familiar with them than the LCWR. Also, it may be that the bishops put forth a clearer Church position, whereas the nuns are often walking a tightrope around the bishops, which can be linked to the institutional maneuvering female religious do to impact social policy. However, because the nuns' positions at times are not as clearly defined (e.g., their messages on inclusiveness toward gay Catholics as opposed to specifically stating they support gay marriage and adoption), it may lead some Catholics not to see them as an opinion leader and reject their messages and cues, as evidenced in the findings presented here. Second, although more deference is given to the bishops (particularly evidenced in the difference of means tests), it does not indicate their influence is uniform among Catholics. And third, as evidenced in the moderating effects, the Catholic Church has an authority problem. Despite the first part of the analysis demonstrating more influence by the bishops, the moderating effects show that those with a predisposition to authority (who we might expect to be aligned with the bishops when presented with their positions), do not necessarily move in the direction of the hierarchy when immediately exposed to their cues and messages. This again is a challenge to the bishops as they work to hold on to traditional positions yet are dealing with a laity that increasingly supports gay rights, birth control access, and other socially progressive positions (Pew Research Center 2016). This also speaks to the Holman and Shockley (2017) argument that Catholics are not a "monolithic" faith group, and, despite existing in a "rigid" structure, the clergy can be limited in terms of influence due to the diverse makeup of their congregants and varied political positions of both the leadership and laity. In the end, Catholics can receive multiple and at times conflicting cues from Church leaders on a range of issues, as the hierarchy tries to influence many topics across the political spectrum.

Overall, we have learned that male and female Catholic religious use different types of authority to affect social policy, with the male clergy relying on the institutional authority of their office and the nuns on the personal authority they derive from their role as female religious and working more closely with the laity. However, unlike previous studies, the research presented here shows that even though women religious have autonomy and freedom outside of the official hierarchy, they make calculated decisions when to cooperate with it and when not to—this is tied to how they maneuver around institutional constraints. Weighing the possible approaches is also tied to what will best achieve their policy objectives, along with the sense of accountability they feel toward the laity, their vocation, and the mission of their congregations (as specified in the *Perfectae Caritatis*).

What also has become clear is that male and female religious leaders represent two different lives of the Church: religious life and the life of the clergy, both of which cannot be separated from gender nor the tension between policy and authority. Interestingly, this study shows that nuns appear to know both of these lives of the Church, most likely because they have had to learn to navigate around them to impact social policy. As Sister Simone Campbell of NETWORK noted, clerical life is very different than religious life. Secular priests and clergy are in administrative positions, running parishes, and concerned about the institutional preservation of the Church, whereas religious life is more centered on carrying out the faith through the mission of their respective orders and congregations, living in community working with the laity and vulnerable. This theme can be seen in the nuns' documents and arguably added to the misperceptions the bishops and the Vatican had toward the LCWR. I believe the nuns, though upset and hurt by the accusations of the Assessment, were acutely aware of this. And, therefore, despite publicly stating disagreement with the rebuke, they consciously decided to be a model for the institutional Church throughout the renewal process by making an effort to approach the bishop delegates with the lessons they learned in living a religious, not clerical life. This is evidenced by Sister Simone's comments on the LCWR and the Assessment, in discussing how the nuns did not engage in oppositional politics with the American bishops assigned to the renewal. Furthermore, the LCWR engaged the Assessment from a place of contemplation and prayer, bringing their "desire for deep listening and respectful dialogue" to the work with the delegate bishops. The nuns expressed that they dialogued with the delegate bishops about their understanding on "critical matters of faith and its practice, religious life and its mission, and the role of a leadership conference of religious" (LCWR 2015). Though a difficult process, the nuns' approach worked—the bishop delegates began to listen to them, as did Pope Francis (Goodstein 2015). The LCWR added that they felt this strategy and their conversations were mutually beneficial to their organization and the clergy. Upon filing the joint report with the CDF and delegate bishops, the LCWR fulfilled the renewal's requirements of having their organizations' bylaws approved, a committee formed to review their publications and programs, along with guidelines for future conference speakers (LCWR 2015).

In considering the future of a religion that is facing not only a clergy shortage but a decrease in the number of nuns and lay Catholics, this study also shows that it is imperative that the Church work to better the relationship between the institutional authority of the hierarchy and the personal authority of the religious (and quite possibly, the laity). In order for the Church to be a religious force with relevance in the public square it needs to be open to various leadership models. This will undoubtedly mean fully living up to Vatican II reforms that were first articulated over fifty years ago. It appears that Pope Francis is trying to encourage this perspective, asking American bishops to act more pastoral as opposed to clerical in their role by encouraging them to connect and dialogue with the laity (*New York Times* 2015). Moreover, as reports show that over 50 percent of U.S. Catholic parish staffs are made up of women, it is becoming apparent that female empowerment in Church leadership is needed and must be more seriously considered (a long-held position as evidenced in the content analyses of Chapters 3 and 4; Burge 2017; Gray, Gautier, and Cidade 2011). In a response to these realities, in August 2016, Pope Francis instituted a commission to study the female diaconate. Consisting of twelve members from religious, clerical, and academic backgrounds, the commission held its first meeting in November 2016 to begin studying the women deacons of the early Church and what a contemporary version might mean for the Church (Vatican Radio 2016).

One of the sisters interviewed for this study has been actively leading the female diaconate movement in the United States and is also supportive of women entering the priesthood. She shared that she felt opening up the diaconate to women would help the clergy shortage, but not enough "to really address the reality that we are really on our way to not having enough priests for every parish." This is important because deacons cannot celebrate mass, though they are permitted to have a liturgical role in the celebration. The sister noted that under the leadership of Pope Francis she believed the Vatican may open ordination to married men. Because the pope is concerned about the pastoral care of the laity, the sister stated this is probably why Pope Francis "moved female deacons up on his priority list" and that "he doesn't want to be elevating men without also doing something to elevate the status of women. It could be that the female diaconate is one way to negotiating this awkward political situation that they find themselves in." She further shared that one of the major issues surrounding the female diaconate is whether these women would be ordained and part of the permanent diaconate that came out of Vatican II.[1] This sister shared that instead women may be assigned to a minor diaconate or lesser role because the Vatican is worried that if they "ordain women to the order of deacons, equivalent to the way we ordinate male deacons, then you're going to have a harder time making the argument that women can't be priests. That's what they're worried about, regardless." She felt that though the female diaconate could afford additional opportunities for women religious the biggest impact would be experienced by lay Catholic women working in parishes, pointing out that 80 percent of the thirty thousand ecclesial ministers in the American Church are female.

However, Pope Francis has experienced some resistance from conservative American bishops, as well as clergy within the Vatican, who are skeptical of his attempts to democratize the Church and make it more welcoming for all. They appear especially critical of his remarks that the bishops have been "obsessed" with issues pertaining to homosexuality, abortion, and contraception, encouraging them not to talk about these topics all the time and to try to strike a balance in their dialogue with the laity (Goodstein 2013).

This message by Pope Francis parallels the approach and focus of the LCWR regarding these issues and how living a religious life in the Church is a different model for the institution. It is clear that Pope Francis understood this, despite reaffirming the Church's positions against women in the priesthood and making controversial remarks about females more generally. Pope Francis appears to see the need for the clergy to empower women, if the Church wishes to continue to serve the laity and also influence social policy. However, some argue that his recent effort to examine the role of women in the Church is still rooted in theological paradigms that limit women from attaining full equality in the faith and institution (Manson 2016; McElwee 2016). Some pose the question of why would women stay or look to take a greater part in a Church that seems to be apathetic or opposed to their leadership? As Heidi Schlumpf (2015) and other Catholic female scholars argue, not only do some women stay for the strong pull to the sacraments and respect for the Church's rich history but the desire to push for change and empowerment by working inside the institution. As Sister Simone Campbell stated, the Assessment, though painful, showed the strong and positive impact that female religious leadership can have among the laity and within the Church. Though as this study shows there is still resistance to Catholic female leadership, one could argue that the Assessment also reignited a larger conversation about not just issues of social justice but women's role in the Church. Therefore, as the Church continues to evolve in contemporary society, experience growing pains, and deal with the tension of policy and authority between male and female religious it now has the opportunity to fully live out the reforms of Vatican II by empowering women (both lay and religious). As the data show, women are the ones administering the day-to-day life of parishes, influencing policy as evidenced by their work on health care as well as other social justice issues. Regardless of institutional resistance, the future of the Church is female.

Appendix

CHAPTERS 3 AND 4: HAND-CODING SCHEMES

Topic: Economics

1. Is there a particular economic issue the message/statement is addressing?
   a. Affordable housing
   b. Economic justice
   c. Overconsumption
   d. Predatory lending
   e. Other____________________
2. Is one message emphasized more than others? If Yes, which one?
   a. Yes____________________
   b. No
3. Does the message/statement take a stance? If so, what is the stance?
4. Is Catholic social teaching mentioned to support a position taken by an organization?
   a. Yes
   b. No
5. Regarding the general role of government involvement with the economy, what does the article favor?
   a. Regulation
   b. Limited regulation
   c. Spending/taxation
   d. Larger role of government
   e. Call for religious leadership
   f. Other___________
   g. None

6. Does the message address a particular population or demographic?
   a. Yes
   b. No
7. If the answer to question 6 is Yes, which population/demographic is addressed?
   a. Women and/or children
   b. Poor
   c. Immigrants
   d. Other _______
8. Mobilization frame:
   a. Petition government
   b. Contact Catholic politician
   c. Self-reflection/prayer
   d. Home-centered activity
   e. Volunteer
   f. Other_______________________
   g. None

Topic: Immigration

1. Is there a particular immigration issue the message/statement is addressing?
   a. Enforcement, national security, border security
   b. Earned citizenship
   c. Liberalize immigration reform
   d. Family separation and unification
   e. Other_______________________
2. Is one message emphasized more than others? If Yes, which one?
   a. Yes_______________________
   b. No
3. Does the message/statement take a stance on this topic? If so, what is the stance?
4. Is Catholic social teaching mentioned to support a position taken by an organization?
   a. Yes
   b. No
5. Regarding general federal involvement with immigration, what does the article favor?
   a. Regulation
   b. Limited regulation
   c. Larger role of government
   d. Call for religious leadership
   e. Other_________
   f. None
6. Does the message address a particular population or demographic?
   a. Yes
   b. No

7. If the answer to question 6 is Yes, which population/demographic is addressed?
   a. Women and/or children
   b. Children
   c. Families
   d. Low economic, poor
   e. Minorities
   f. Religious workers
   g. Immigrants/migrants
   h. Other _______
8. Mobilization frame:
   a. Petition government
   b. Contact Catholic politician
   c. Self-reflection/prayer
   d. Home-centered activity
   e. Volunteer
   f. Other_______________________
   g. None

Topic: Death Penalty

1. Is there a particular frame or approach the message takes to the death penalty?
   a. Yes
   b. No
2. If yes, which of the following frames/approaches does the message take on the death penalty?
   a. Focuses on racial or class bias
   b. Cost/financial impact
   c. Moral, dignity for human life (moral reasoning to call for end of death penalty)
   d. Abolition (call to end the death penalty)
   e. Juvenile death penalty
3. Is one message emphasized more than others? If Yes, which one?
   a. Yes_______________________
   b. No
4. Does the message/statement take a stance/position on the death penalty? If so, what is the stance?
5. Is Catholic social teaching mentioned to support a position taken by an organization?
   a. Yes
   b. No
   c. None
6. Does the message address a particular population or demographic? If yes, which population?
   a. Yes_______________________
   b. No

7. If the answer to question 6 is Yes, which population/demographic is addressed?
   a. Adults
   b. Juveniles
   c. Race/ethnicity
   d. Class
8. Mobilization frame:
   a. Petition government
   b. Contact Catholic politician
   c. Self-reflection/prayer
   d. Home-centered activity
   e. Volunteer
   f. Other______________________
   g. None

Topic: Environment

1. Is there a particular environmental issue the message/statement is addressing?
   a. Climate change
   b. Environmental degradation
   c. Overconsumption
   d. Other___________
2. Does the message/statement take a stance on the topic? If so, what is the stance?
3. Is Catholic social teaching mentioned to support a position taken by an organization?
   a. Yes
   b. No
4. Regarding the general role of government involvement with the environment, what does the article favor?
   a. Larger, more regulation
   b. Limited regulation
   c. Spending/taxation
   d. Call for religious leadership
   e. Other_________
   f. None
5. Which frame/concept of environment and gender is discussed?
   a. Environmental degradation
   b. Environmental risk
   c. Ecological feminism
   d. Environmental justice
6. Does the message address a particular population or demographic?
   a. Yes
   b. No

7. If the answer to question 6 is Yes, which population/demographic is addressed?
   a. Women and/or children
   b. Poor
   c. Other _______
8. Mobilization frame:
   a. Petition government
   b. Contact Catholic politician
   c. Self-reflection/prayer
   d. Home-centered activity
   e. Volunteer
   f. Other_______________________
   g. None

Topic: Health Care

1. Is there a particular health care issue the message/statement is addressing?
   a. Affordable health care reform
   b. Health Human Service Mandate and/or reproductive health care services
   c. Federally funded abortion
   d. Refusal clauses/conscience protection/freedom of conscience
2. Is one message emphasized more than others? If Yes, which one?
   a. Yes_______________________
   b. No
3. Does the message/statement take a stance? If so, what is the stance?
4. Is Catholic social teaching mentioned to support a position taken by an organization?
   a. Yes
   b. No
5. Regarding the general federal involvement with health care, what does the article favor?
   a. Regulation
   b. Limited regulation
   c. Spending/taxation
   d. Larger role of government
   e. Call for religious leadership
   f. Other__________
   g. None
6. Does the message address a particular population or demographic?
   a. Yes
   b. No
7. If the answer to question 6 is Yes, which population/demographic is addressed?
   a. Women and/or children
   b. Poor

c. Minorities
d. Immigrants
e. Other __________
f. None

8. Mobilization frame:
a. Petition government
b. Contact Catholic politician
c. Self-reflection/prayer
d. Home-centered activity
e. Volunteer
f. Other______________________
g. None

Topic: Homosexuality

1. Does the message/statement take a stance on the topic? If so, what is the stance?
2. Is Catholic social teaching mentioned to support a position taken by an organization?
a. Yes
b. No
3. Circle "yes" or "no" for the following questions:
a. Is supportive of homosexuality or alternative sexual ethic? Yes or No
b. Against same-sex unions of any kind? Yes or No
c. Is supportive of gay adoption? Yes or No
d. Is supportive of inclusiveness of homosexuals in the Church/faith? Yes or No
4. Is natural law used to support an anti-same-sex marriage and anti–gay adoption stance?
a. Yes
b. No
5. Mobilization frame:
a. Petition government
b. Contact Catholic politician
c. Self-reflection/prayer
d. Home-centered activity
e. Volunteer
f. Other______________________
g. None

Topic: Gender Roles

1. What overall view of gender roles does this message/statement have?
a. Progressive
b. Orthodox

2. Is Catholic social teaching mentioned to support a position taken by an organization?
   a. Yes
   b. No
3. Are natural law or themes of nature brought up in describing gender roles?
   a. Yes
   b. No
4. If gender roles are mentioned, what frame/rationale is used?
   a. Roles based on gender
   b. Emphasis on mother and/or wife
   c. Female leadership at diocesan level
   d. Female leadership in hierarchy
   e. Egalitarian gender roles in society
   f. Women's empowerment
5. Mobilization frame:
   a. Petition government
   b. Contact Catholic politician
   c. Self-reflection/prayer
   d. Home-centered activity
   e. Volunteer
   f. Other______________________
   g. None

CHAPTER 5: EXPERIMENTAL TREATMENT STATEMENTS BY TOPIC

Note, as discussed in Chapter 5, the control group did not receive statements but did receive questions. These same treatments were also used in Chapter 6.

Topic: Homosexuality

Treatment for USCCB (Bishops) Groups

Treatment Group A knew the following statement was from the USCCB; Treatment Group B did not know the source cue.

Ministry to Persons with a Homosexual Inclination: Guidelines for Pastoral Care, November 14, 2006:

> The Church recognizes that "marriage exists solely between a man and a woman, who by mutual personal gift, proper and exclusive to themselves, tend toward the communion of their persons. In this way, they mutually perfect each other, in order to cooperate with God in the procreation and upbringing of new human lives." Consequently, the Church does not support so-called same-sex "marriages" or any semblance thereof, including civil unions that give the appearance of marriage. Church ministers may not bless such unions or promote

> them in any way, directly or indirectly. Summarily, the Church does not support the adoption of children by same-sex couples since homosexual unions are contrary to the divine plan.

Treatment for LCWR (Nuns) Group

Treatment Group C knew the following statement was from the LCWR; Treatment Group D did not know the source cue.

Annual Assembly Presidential Address, Tending the Holy through the Power of Sisterhood, August 22, 2003:

> During one meeting, our conversation turned to a discussion of the church's position on homosexuality. As some of the participants made their appeal to ethical directives based in natural law and the intrinsically disordered nature of homosexuality, I found myself tapping into a place of grief and alienation. In my heart's eye, I saw faces of men and women I know whose sexual orientation is gay or lesbian and who live compassionately, justly yearning for a return of compassion and justice on the part of a church they love. I thought of men and women whose passion for wholeness in relationship is lived in deep commitment to lifelong same-sex partners. I heard deep in my own being, their struggle to find a home in our church.

Posttreatment Questions on the Topic of Homosexuality

Self-identification: How one identifies one's sexual orientation (gay, lesbian, bisexual, or heterosexual). Taken from "Best Practices for Asking Questions about Sexual Orientation on Surveys," The Williams Institute, 2009, 9–14.

Wording: Do you consider yourself to be:

1. Heterosexual or straight
2. Gay or lesbian
3. Bisexual

Gay Marriage: One's support/opposition for gay marriage.

Wording: To what extent do you support or oppose gay marriage?

1. Strongly support
2. Support
3. Somewhat support
4. Neither support nor oppose
5. Somewhat oppose
6. Oppose
7. Strongly oppose

Gay adoption: Position on homosexual couples adopting children.

Wording: Do you support or oppose gay or lesbian couples being permitted to adopt children?

1. Strongly support
2. Support

3. Somewhat support
4. Neither support nor oppose
5. Somewhat oppose
6. Oppose
7. Strongly oppose

Choice of Being Homosexual: Position on if homosexuality is something that can be chosen or cannot change. Taken from the 1993 American National Election Survey Pilot Study, March 16, 1994.

Wording: Do you think being homosexual is something people choose to be, or do you think it is something they cannot change?

1. Choose
2. Don't know
3. People cannot change

Topic: Gender Roles

Treatment for USCCB (Bishops) Group

Treatment Group A knew the following statement was from the USCCB; Treatment Group B did not know the source cue.

Statement, Ten Frequently Asked Questions about the Reservation of Priestly Ordination to Men:

> The Church cannot consider the claim of a woman that God has called her to ordained ministry because the very possibility of priestly ordination arises only within the framework of a divine plan and order in which participation in Christ's role as head of the Church is reserved to men. . . . The holy women who form such an important part of the gospel story, beginning with the Blessed Virgin Mary, clearly had a different role to play, and in that they have been followed by other women down through the ages in ways appropriate to the time and place.

Treatment for LCWR (Nuns) Group

Treatment Group C knew the following statement was from the LCWR; Treatment Group D did not know the source cue.

Keynote Address at Annual Assembly, What Can Religious Bring to Globalization? by Mary Robinson, August 2004:

> The infringement of women's rights is usually exercised in the name of tradition, religion, social cohesion, morality, or some complex of transcendent values. Women from different cultures must be prepared to create that vital space for women to determine their own priorities. Women must be enabled to participate fully and equally in decision making within the faiths themselves, and their concerns need to be embraced as priorities in prayer, advocacy and activism.

Posttreatment Questions on the Topic of Gender Roles

Women's equal role. Taken from the American National Election Studies 1948 to 2008 Time Series Survey.

Wording: Some people feel that women should have an equal role with men in running business, industry and government. Suppose these people are at one end of a scale, point 1. Others feel that a women's place is in the home. Suppose these people are at the other end; at point 7. And, of course, some people have opinions somewhere in between, at points 2, 3, 4, 5, or 6. Where would you place yourself on this scale?

1. Women and men should have an equal role.
2.
3.
4.
5.
6.
7. Women's place is in the home.

Women and the Catholic Church. Taken from the Pew Research Center, "Changing Faiths: Latinos and the Transformation of American Religion (2006 Hispanic Religion Survey)", August 10, 2006, to October 4, 2006.

Wording: In your opinion, does the Catholic Church in the United States:

1. Respect the contributions of women more than it respects the contributions of men
2. Respect the contributions of both men and women equally
3. Respect the contributions of men more than it respects the contributions of women

Women and the priesthood. Derived from the Pew Research Center February 2014 Political Survey

Wording: To what extent do you agree or disagree with the following statement. The Catholic Church should not allow women to become priests.

1. Strongly agree
2. Agree
3. Somewhat agree
4. Neither agree nor disagree
5. Somewhat disagree
6. Disagree
7. Strongly disagree

Topic: Economics

Treatment for USCCB (Bishops) Group

Treatment Group A knew the following statement was from the USCCB; Treatment Group B did not know the source cue.

Statement on the Federal Budget: Advocating a Circle of Protection, February 2012:

> The federal budget is a moral document reflecting the priorities and values of the nation, and these priorities have consequences on people's lives. In the face of historic deficits, the nation faces unavoidable choices about how to balance needs and resources and allocate burdens and sacrifices. We advocate principles that assure adequate funding for programs that assist those in greatest need who are trying to care for their children, access healthcare, overcome hunger and homelessness and find gainful employment.

Treatment for LCWR (Nuns) Group

Treatment Group C knew the following statement was from the LCWR; Treatment Group D did not know the source cue.

Resolution to Action, Economic Justice Advocacy Critically Needed, Fall 2011:

> We continue to assert that the budget is a moral document and that the spending and revenue outlined therein reflect our nation's values. We strongly support the preferential option for the poor and are, therefore, advocating to ensure that the budget preserves the social safety net so essential to those most in need. Human needs supporters now must fight to protect the structural integrity of entitlement programs and for sufficient overall domestic discretionary funding to ensure the well-being of those most in need. WIC which provides nutritional aid to women, infants and children, Low-Income Home Energy Assistance Program (LIHEAP), and other programs such as these are most at risk in an environment focused on deficit reduction and smaller government.

Posttreatment Questions on the Topic of Economics

Federal Budget/Welfare Spending: One's preference on federal budget and welfare spending. Taken from the American National Election Studies 1948 to 2008 Time Series Survey.

Wording: If you had a say in making up the federal budget this year, would you like to see spending increase, stay the same, or decrease for welfare programs?

1. Increase
2. Same
3. Decrease
4. Cut out entirely

Federal Budget/Spending on the Poor: One's preference on federal budget and spending on the poor. Taken from the American National Election Studies 1948 to 2008 Time Series Survey.

Wording: If you had a say in making up the federal budget this year, would you like to see spending increase, stay the same, or decrease in aid to the poor?

1. Increase
2. Same
3. Decrease
4. Cut out entirely

Role of Government/Standard of Living: One's position on whether or not the government should ensure a good standard of living. Taken from the American National Election Studies 1948 to 2008 Time Series Survey.

Wording: Some people feel the government should see to it that every person has a job and a good standard of living. Others think the government should just let each person get ahead on their own. Which is closer to the way you feel or do you not know?

1. The government should see to it that every person has a job and a good standard of living.
2.
3.
4.
5.
6.
7. The government should just let each person get ahead on their own.

Topic: Environment

Treatment for USCCB (Bishops) Group

Treatment Group A knew the following statement was from the USCCB; Treatment Group B did not know the source cue.

Statement on Climate Change, Faithful Stewards of God's Creation—A Catholic Resource for Environmental Justice and Climate Change, 2001:

> Today, our Catholic community is addressing more consistently and faithfully how to protect God's creation and the environment that sustains the human family and all the earth. As Pope John Paul II said, "respect for life and for the dignity of the human person extends also to the rest of creation, which is called to join man in praising God." We show our respect for our Creator by our care for His creation. Today, there is a particular and pressing responsibility to examine and act on the growing challenge of global climate change and its implications for God's creation and for the poor and vulnerable. During his angelus address on August 27, 2006, Pope Benedict XVI called for a commitment to care for creation. He said creation is "exposed to serious risks by life choices and lifestyles that can degrade it." In particular, he said, "environmental degradation makes the lives of the poor especially unbearable."

Treatment for LCWR (Nuns) Group

Treatment Group C knew the following statement was from the LCWR; Treatment Group D did not know the source cue.

Resolution to Action, Climate Change and Hunger, January 2009:

> Most heart wrenching is the report of a West African mother; desperate to provide for the family, she sold four of her children. The $64 she received helped her feed the rest awhile longer. Estimates are that one billion people will go hungry and another two billion will be undernourished and 16,000 children die of hunger related causes every day. . . . Blame is cast upon high fuel prices which heighten costs of transportation, agricultural inputs, and commercially produced crops; increased production and use of biofuels; rising demand for energy and a varied, higher animal protein diet among populations in emerging economies; national and international trade and agricultural policies; commodity market speculations; more frequent floods, droughts, and poor harvests; climate change. Climate change is a key factor in the increased hunger in the world. . . . Poor people and countries who have contributed least to climate change suffer the worst impacts and are particularly affected by the negative consequences.

Posttreatment Questions on the Topic of the Environment

Environmental Regulation. Taken from the American National Election Studies 1948 to 2008 Time Series Survey.

Wording: Some people think that current regulations to protect the environment are already too much of a burden on business. Suppose these people are at one end of a scale, point 1. Other people think we need much tougher government regulations on business in order to protect the environment. Suppose these people are at the other end of the scale at point 7. And, of course, some other people have opinions somewhere in between, at points 2, 3, 4, 5, or 6. Where would you place yourself on this scale?

1. Much tougher regulations are needed to protect the environment
2.
3.
4.
5.
6.
7. Regulations are already too much of a burden on business

Environment and target population. Derived to gauge respondents' knowledge of environmental feminism.

Wording: To what extent do you agree or disagree that the topic of the environment a feminist issue?

1. Strongly agree
2. Agree
3. Somewhat agree
4. Neither agree nor disagree
5. Somewhat disagree

6. Disagree
7. Strongly disagree

Spiritual/Religious Views on Climate Change/Environment. Derived to gauge respondents' belief in a religious or moral obligation to the environment. Taken from Siegel, Jonas, 2012, "Religious Views on Climate Change and Mitigation," Center for International and Security Studies at Maryland.

Wording: To what extent do you agree or disagree that people have a spiritual obligation to be responsible stewards of God's creation, in our actions and in supporting the actions of others who work to protect the environment?

1. Strongly agree
2. Agree
3. Somewhat agree
4. Neither agree nor disagree
5. Somewhat disagree
6. Disagree
7. Strongly disagree

Assessing threat posed by climate change. Designed to gauge respondent's views of climate change.

Wording: To what extent do you agree or disagree that climate change poses a serious threat to people around the world?

1. Strongly agree
2. Agree
3. Somewhat agree
4. Neither agree nor disagree
5. Somewhat disagree
6. Disagree
7. Strongly disagree

CHAPTER 5: VARIABLES AND CODING

Age

1=18–24
2=25–35
3=36–45
4=46–55
5=56–65
6=over 65

Sex

1=Male
0=Female

Race/Ethnicity

*(note that each racial/ethnic category is its own variable and was coded 1 if the subjected responded for that race/ethnic category and 0 if not):

White
Black
Hispanic
Asian
Other

Income

1=$14,999 or less
2=$15,000–$29,999
3=$30,000–$49,999
4=$50,000–$74,999
5=$75,000–$99,999
6=$100,000 or more

Party ID

1=Republican
2=Democrat
3=Independent
4=Something else

Education

1=Did not complete high school
2=Completed high school or equivalent
3=Some college
4=College graduate
5=Some graduate school
6=Completed graduate school

Predisposition to Authority Battery

1=Obey; 0=Question
1=Rules; 0=Progress
1=Obedience; 0=Curiosity
1=Obey parents; 0=Responsible for own action
1=Respect elders; 0=Thinks for themselves
1=Good manners; 0=Good sense/sound judgment

Notes

CHAPTER 1

I would like to note that this analysis is a result of my scholarly examination, evaluation, and findings of the Doctrinal Assessment of the LCWR, along with the influence of male clergy and female religious within the American Catholic Church. I do not speak for any of the organizations discussed and examined in this book.

1. Catholic social teaching is a body of doctrine developed by the Catholic Church on matters of social justice, which include issues of poverty, economics, wealth, and the role of social organizations and the state. The development of this body of doctrine began with *Rerum Novarum* (1891), an encyclical by Pope Leo XIII, and has been at the core of Catholic faith and teaching since then (United States Conference of Catholic Bishops 2010; *Catechism of the Catholic Church* 2010a).

2. Information from an author interview of a representative from the LCWR, February 29, 2016.

3. Ibid.

4. Information from an author interview of a representative from NETWORK, February 18, 2016.

5. Ibid.

6. Vatican II was first convened under Pope John XXIII in 1962. In 1963, Pope John XXIII died and the council continued under the newly elected pontiff, Pope Paul VI, until its conclusion in 1965 (Libreria Editrice Vaticana). Accessed August 12, 2017; available at http://www.vatican.va/archive/hist_councils/ii_vatican_council/documents/vat-ii_decree_19651028_perfectae-caritatis_en.html.

CHAPTER 2

1. The CMSWR is a collaborative body of women religious. It comprises major superiors and assistants of religious congregations. Available at http://cmswr.org/about/mission-vision-core-values. Future Church is an organization that works for more inclusion and collaboration within the Catholic Church, along with the advancement of leadership for women. Available at https://www.futurechurch.org/about-ushttps://www.futurechurch.org/about-ushttps://www.futurechurch.org/about-us. Websites accessed August 12, 2017.

2. The CMSM is a leadership organization of male religious in the United States. Available at http://www.cmsm.org/about.shtml. Accessed August 12, 2017.

3. This is part of the American Psychological Association's description of civic engagement. Available at http://www.apa.org/education/undergrad/civic-engagement.aspx. Accessed August 12, 2017.

4. Information on the ruling is available at http://thefederalist.com/2016/05/16/supreme-court-opinion-a-win-for-the-little-sisters-of-the-poor/. Accessed August 12, 2017.

5. Statement on behalf of the USCCB on the Barack Obama administration and Universal Health Care. Available at http://www.usccb.org/_cs_upload/8096_1.pdf. Accessed August 12, 2017.

6. "Text of Nun's Letter Endorsing Obamacare." Available at http://www.cathmed.org/assets/files/LCWR%20Letter.pdf. Accessed August 12, 2017.

CHAPTER 3

1. In order to control for intercoder reliability, two trained research coders also assisted in separately and independently coding the entire sample of documents, which consisted of 188 statements (125 from the USCCB and 63 from the LCWR) from the time period of 2000 to 2012.

The results for each coder were run through SPSS, and a Cronbach's Alpha test was conducted to measure reliability and internal consistency on mobilization activity. The results for the organizations priorities reported a Cronbach's Alpha score of 0.759 and 0.60 for type of mobilization activity. Both of these scores signaled that intercoder reliability was successfully achieved (Landis and Koch 1977; Landers 2011).

2. Total statements per organization: USCCB, 125; LCWR, 63.

3. In 1994, Pope John Paul II stated "I declare that the Church has no authority whatsoever to confer priestly ordination on women and that this judgment is to be definitively held by all the Church's faithful" (*Ordinatio Sacerdotalis* 4). Available at http://www.vatican.va/holy_father/john_paul_ii/apost_letters/documents/hf_jp-ii_apl_22051994_ordinatio-sacerdotalis_en.html.

4. *Ordinatio Sacerdotalis* is an Apostolic Letter issued by Pope John Paul II on May 24, 1994, explaining the institutional position that the "Church has no authority whatsoever to confer priestly ordination on women" (Vatican 1994). Available at https://w2.vatican.va/content/john-paul-ii/en/apost_letters/1994

/documents/hf_jp-ii_apl_19940522_ordinatio-sacerdotalis.html. Accessed August 14, 2017.

CHAPTER 4

1. Note that this chapter is a continuation of the content analysis discussed in Chapter 3 and therefore covers the same set of 188 statements from the USCCB and LCWR on the seven topics of environment, homosexuality, health care, economics, the death penalty, immigration, and gender roles.

CHAPTER 5

1. Again, the treatment groups were also designed to capture whether knowing the source cue (meaning which organization issued the statement) had an effect, hence two groups knew the source cues (Group A: Knows USCCB Source Cue, n=209, and Group C: Knows LCWR Source Cue, n=223) and two did not (Group B: Do Not Know USCCB Source Cue, n=232, and Group D: Do Not Know LCWR Source Cue, n=210).

2. It is important to note that the topics analyzed (homosexuality, women's role in society and the Church, government aid to the poor, and the environment) were chosen as a result of the content analysis project discussed in Chapters 3 and 4. It became evident that there were notable differences in the areas of gender roles and homosexuality. Two of the areas in which the organizations had similar positions where the economy (with attention to aid to the poor) and the environment, albeit each used different concept frames of emphasis. Thus, as part of the larger project studying these two organizations, this chapter maintains continuity by examining the same topics.

3. Demographic variables showed means and standard deviation scores that were consistent across treatment groups, along with insignificant chi-square scores indicating that the sample was balanced in composition across the treatment and control groups. The only variable that did not show this was marital status, with a chi-squared p=.026.

4. The national averages on Catholics are from the Pew Research Center's Forum on Religion and Public Life, U.S. Religious Landscape Survey Religious Affiliation: Diverse and Dynamic. February 2008. Available at http://religions.pewforum.org/pdf/report-religious-landscape-study-full.pdf.

5. In looking at the results in tables 5.2, 5.3, and 5.4, the variable "Authority" (auth1) in the first column represents those that are predisposed to authority, so auth1=1 and the control or treatment group=0. When looking at the second column, the coefficient for "Group" (representing either the control of one of the treatment groups), treatment=1 and auth1=0. Finally, when looking at the third column, the interaction "Group*Authority" (again representing either the con trol or one of the treatment groups interacted with auth1/"Authority"), control or treatment=1 and auth1=1.

6. Reflects order listed in first column of table 5.2: p=.001, p=.000, p=.000, p=.003, p=.000.

CHAPTER 6

1. The permanent diaconate permitted married men to become deacons, no longer primarily reserving it to seminarians who were making this transitionary step on their way to becoming priests. The ministry of a deacon is rooted in service to the parish, and, therefore, they usually perform tasks assigned by the pastor of the Church or bishop of the diocese. Deacons are considered ordained clerics and have a liturgical role in the liturgy and therefore can preach, along with conducting baptism and marriages. Accessed August 17, 2017. Available at http://canonlawmadeeasy.com/2013/09/26/what-can-and-cant-a-deacon-do/.

References

Acker, Joan. 1990. "Hierarchies, Jobs, Bodies: A Theory of Gendered Organizations." *Gender and Society* 4(2): 139–158.

Adams, Jimi. 2007. "Stained Glass Makes the Ceiling Visible Organizational Opposition to Women in Congregational Leadership." *Gender and Society* 21(1): 80–105.

Altemeyer, Bob. 1981. *Right-Wing Authoritarianism*. Winnipeg: University of Manitoba Press.

———. 1988. *Enemies of Freedom: Understanding Right-Wing Authoritarianism*. San Francisco, CA: Jossey-Bass.

———. 1996. *The Authoritarian Specter*. Cambridge, MA: Harvard University Press.

ANES (American National Election Studies). 1993. "Survey Polite Study." Accessed March 16, 2014. Available at https://electionstudies.org/data-center/.

———. 2008. "1948 to 2008 Time Series Survey." Accessed March 16, 2014. Available at https://electionstudies.org/data-center/.

Arceneaux, Kevin. 2008. "Can Partisan Cues Diminish Accountability?" *Political Behavior* 30(2): 139–160.

Arceneaux, Kevin, and Robin Kolodny. 2009. "Educating the Least Informed: Group Endorsements in a Grassroots Campaign." *American Journal of Political Science* 53(4): 755–770.

Arnold, R. Douglas. 1993. "Can Inattentive Citizens Control Their Elected Representatives?" In *Congress Reconsidered*, ed. Lawrence C. Dodd and Bruce I. Oppenheimer, 401–416. Washington, DC: CQ Press.

Awamleh, Raed, and William L. Gardner. 1999. "Perceptions of Leader Charisma and Effectiveness: The Effects of Vision Content, Delivery, and Organizational Performance." *Leadership Quarterly* 10(3): 345–373.

Baggett, Jerome P. 2006. "The Catholic Citizen: Perennial Puzzle or Emergent Oxymoron?" *Social Compass* 53(2): 291–309.

Bakalar, Nicholas. 2017. "Nearly 20 Million Have Gained Health Insurance since 2010." *New York Times*, May 22. Accessed November 18, 2017. Available at https://www.nytimes.com/2017/05/22/health/obamacare-health-insurance-numbers-nchs.html.

Bartels, Larry M. 2002. "Beyond the Running Tally: Partisan Bias in Political Perceptions." *Political Behavior* 24(2): 117–150.

Bauman, Michelle. 2013. "The LCWR vs. the Vatican: Setting the Record Straight." *National Catholic Register*, May 17. Accessed June 1, 2016. Available at http://www.ncregister.com/daily-news/the-lcwr-vs.-the-vatican-setting-the-record-straight/#ixzz2frzaojKi.

Beaman, L. G. 2001. "Molly Mormons, Mormon Feminists, and Moderates: Religious Diversity and the LDS Church." *Sociology of Religion* 62(1): 65–86.

Berrelleza, Erick, Mary L. Gautier, and Mark M. Gray. 2014. "Population Trends among Religious Institutes of Women." *Center for Applied Research in the Apostolate*. Accessed March 8, 2017. Available at https://cara.georgetown.edu/wp-content/uploads/2018/06/Women_Religious_Fall2014_FINAL.pdf.

Berry, Jason. 2012. "A New Inquisition: The Vatican Targets US Nuns." *Public Radio International*, December 18. Accessed July 24, 2017. Available at https://www.pri.org/stories/2012-12-18/new-inquisition-vatican-targets-us-nuns.

Bjarnason, Thoroddur, and Michael R. Welch. 2004. "Father Knows Best: Parishes, Priests, and American Catholic Parishioners' Attitudes towards Capital Punishment." *Journal for the Scientific Study of Religion* 43(1): 103–118.

Bligh, Michelle, Jeffery C. Kholes, and James R. Meindl. 2004. "Charisma under Crisis: Presidential Leadership, Rhetoric, and Media Responses before and after the September 11th Terrorist Attacks." *Leadership Quarterly* 15(2): 211–239.

Bligh, Michelle, Jennifer Merolla, and Jean Reith Schroedel. 2010. "Finding Her Voice: Hillary Clinton's Rhetoric in the 2008 Presidential Campaign." *Women's Studies: An Inter-Disciplinary Journal* 39(8): 823–850.

Boudreau, Cheryl. 2009. "Closing the Gap: When Do Cues Eliminate Differences between Sophisticated and Unsophisticated Citizens?" *Journal of Politics* 71(3): 964–976.

Bradley Hagerty, Barbara. 2012. "Sisters and Vatican II: A Generational Tug of War." National Public Radio, October 10. Accessed February 1, 2015. Available at http://www.npr.org/2012/10/10/162650803/sisters-and-vatican-ii-a-generational-tug-of-war.

Brady, Henry E., and Paul M. Sniderman. 1985. "Attitude Attribution: A Group Basis for Political Reasoning." *American Political Science Review* 79(4): 1061–1107.

Brigham, Erin. 2015. "Women Religious and the Public Voice of Catholicism." *Journal of Feminist Studies in Religion* 31(2): 109–126.

Burge, Ryan. 2017. "Who's Afraid of Female Clergy?" *Religion in Public: Exploring the Mix of Sacred and Secular*, October 25. Accessed October 27, 2017. Available at https://religioninpublic.blog/2017/10/25/whos-afraid-of-female-clergy/.

Burns, Gene 1992. *The Frontiers of Catholicism: The Politics of Ideology in a Liberal World*. Berkeley: University of California Press.

Byrnes, Timothy A. 1993. "The Politics of American Catholic Hierarchy." *Political Science Quarterly* 108(3): 497–514.

Calfano, Brian, and Elizabeth Oldmixon. 2016. "Remembering to Ask the Boss: Priming and the Dynamics of Priest Reliance on Bishop Cues." *Religions* 7(3): 1–18.

Calfano, Brian, Elizabeth Oldmixon, and Mark Gray. 2014. "Strategically Prophetic Priests: An Analysis of Competing Principal Influence on Clergy Political Action." *Review of Religious Research* 56(1): 1–21.

Calvert, Randall L. 1985. "The Value of Biased Information: A Rational Choice Model of Political Advice." *Journal of Politics* 47(2): 530–555.

Campbell, David E. 2004. "Acts of Faith: Churches and Political Engagement." *Political Behavior* 26(2): 155–180.

CARA (Center for Applied Research in the Apostolate). 2005. "Understanding the Ministry and Experience: Parish Life Coordinators in the United States." Accessed January 9, 2017. Available at http://cara.georgetown.edu/product/understanding-the-ministry-and-experience-parish-life-coordinators-in-the-united-states-summer-2005/.

———. 2017. "Frequently Requested Church Statistics." Accessed February 4, 2017. Available at http://cara.georgetown.edu/frequently-requested-church-statistics/.

Carey, Ann. 2015. "LCWR Agrees to Abide by Vatican's Corrections." *National Catholic Register*, April 16. Accessed July 8, 2017. Available at http://www.ncregister.com/daily-news/lcwr-agrees-to-abide-by-vaticans-corrections.

Carroll, Jackson W. 1981. "Some Issues in Clergy Authority." *Review of Religious Research* 23(2): 99–117.

Catechism of the Catholic Church, 2nd ed. 2010. Vatican: Libreria Editrice Vaticana.

Catholic Answers. 2011. "What Is the Difference between Secular Priests and Religious Priests?" August 4. Accessed August 29, 2017. Available at https://www.catholic.com/qa/what-is-the-difference-between-secular-priests-and-religious-priests.

Catholic Medical Association. 2010. "Text of Nun's Letter Endorsing Obamacare." Accessed July 8, 2017. Available at http://www.cathmed.org/assets/files/LCWR%20Letter.pdf.

"Catholic Share Bishops' Concerns about Religious Liberty." 2012. Pew Research Center Religion and Public Life, August 1. Accessed November 18, 2017. Available at http://www.pewforum.org/2012/08/01/2012-catholic-voters-religious-liberty-issue/#views-of-catholic-leaders.

Cavendish, James C. 2001. "To March or Not to March: Clergy Mobilization Strategies and Grassroots Antidrug Activism." In *Christian Clergy in American Politics*, ed. Sue E. S. Crawford and Laura R. Olson, 203–226. Baltimore, MD: John Hopkins University Press.

Charlton, J. 1997. "Clergywomen of the Pioneer Generation: A Longitudinal Study." *Journal for the Scientific Study of Religion* 36(4): 599–613.

———. 2000. "Women and Clergywomen." *Sociology of Religion* 61(4): 419–424.

Chaves, Mark. 1997. *Ordaining Women: Culture and Conflict in Religious Organizations*. Cambridge, MA: Harvard University Press.

Chaves, Mark, and James D. Montgomery. 1996. "Rationality and the Framing of Religious Choices." *Journal for the Scientific Study of Religion* 35(2): 128–144.

Chliwniak, Luba. 1997. "Higher Education Leadership: Analyzing the Gender Gap." *ASHE-ERIC Higher Education Report* 25:4. Washington, DC: The George Washington University, Graduate School of Education and Human Development.

Clark, Marge. 2011. "Economic Justice Advocacy Critically Needed." *Resolution to Action* 20(3): 1–3. Accessed July 8, 2017. Available at https://lcwr.org/sites/default/files/publications/files/RTA11-11.pdf.

Cohen, Geoffrey L. 2003. "Party over Policy: The Dominating Impact of Group Influence on Political Beliefs." *Journal of Personality and Social Psychology* 85(5): 808–822.

Crawford, Sue E. S., and Laura R. Olson, eds. 2001. *Christian Clergy in American Politics*. Baltimore, MD: John Hopkins University Press.

Deckman, Melissa M., Sue E. S. Crawford, Laura R. Olson, and John C. Green. 2003. "Clergy and the Politics of Gender: Women and Political Opportunity in Mainline Protestant Churches." *Journal for the Scientific Study of Religion* 42(4): 621–632.

DICTON 6.0 Help Manual. 2012. Digitext, Inc.

Djupe, Paul A., and Brian R. Calfano. 2012. "The Deliberative Pulpit: The Democratic Norms and Practices of the PCUSA." *Journal for the Scientific Study of Religion* 51(1): 90–109.

———. 2014. *God Talk: Experimenting with the Religious Causes of Public Opinion*. Philadelphia: Temple University Press.

Djupe, Paul A., and Christopher P. Gilbert. 2002. "The Political Voice of Clergy." *Journal of Politics* 64:596–609.

———. 2009. *The Political Influence of Churches*. Cambridge: Cambridge University Press.

Djupe, Paul A., and Jacob R. Neiheisel. 2008. "Clergy Deliberation on Gay Rights and Homosexuality." *Polity* 40(4): 411–435.

Djupe, Paul A., and Laura R. Olson. 2013. "Stained-glass Politics and Descriptive Representation: Does Associational Leadership by Women Engender Political Engagement among Women?" *Politics, Groups and Identities* 1(3): 329–348.

Dodson, Deborah L., and Susan J. Carroll. 1991. *Reshaping the Agenda: Women in State Legislatures*. New Brunswick: State University of New Jersey.

Donahue, Karen. 2006. "Opposition to the Death Penalty." *Resolutions to Action* 15(2). Accessed February 1, 2015. Available at https://lcwr.org/sites/default/files/publications/files/RTA4-06.pdf.

Druckman, James N. 2001a. "On the Limits of Framing Effects: Who Can Frame?" *Journal of Politics* 63(4): 1041–1066.

———. 2001b. "The Implications of Framing Effects for Citizen Competence." *Political Behavior* 23(3): 225–256.

Druckman, James N., Cari Lynn Hennessy, Kristi St. Charles, and Jonathan Webber. 2010. "Competing Rhetoric over Time: Frames versus Cues." *Journal of Politics* 72(1): 136–148.

Dufour, L. R. 2000. "Sifting through Tradition: The Creation of Jewish Feminist Identities." *Journal for the Scientific Study of Religion* 39(1): 90–106.

Duin, Julia. 2009. "Vatican Probes Nuns' Heterodoxy." *Washington Times*, April 20. Accessed August 29, 2017. Available at https://www.washingtontimes.com/news/2009/apr/20/vatican-probes-nuns-lack-of-adherence-to-doctrine/.

Dwyer, Sara, Catherine Pinkerton, and Marge Clark. 2008. "2008 Elections: From 'YOYO' to 'WITT' Economics. Leadership Conference of Women Religious." *Resolutions to Action* 17(1). Accessed February 1, 2015. Available at https://lcwr.org/sites/default/files/publications/files/RTA1-08.pdf.

Eagly, Alice, and Shelly Chaiken. 1993. *The Psychology of Attitudes*. Fort Worth, TX: Harcourt Brace.

Ebaugh, Helen Rose. 1993. "Patriarchal Bargains and Latent Avenues of Social Mobility: Nuns in the Roman Catholic Church." *Gender and Society* 7(3): 400–414.

Eidenmuller, Michael E. 2002. "American Evangelicalism, Democracy, and Civic Piety: A Computer-Based Stylistic Analysis of Promise Keepers' Stadium Event and Washington DC Rally Discourses." *Journal of Communication and Religion* 25(1): 64–85.

"Female and Catholic: An Interview with Sister Mary Luke Tobin, S.L." 1984. *U.S. Catholic Faith in Real Life*. Accessed July 8, 2017. Available at http://www.uscatholic.org/church/2012/09/female-and-catholic-interview-sister-mary-luke-tobin-sl.

Finlay, B. 1996. "Do Men and Women Have Different Goals for Ministry? Evidence from Seminarians." *Sociology of Religion* 57(3): 311–318.

Fiorenza, Elisabeth S. 2002. "Public Discourse, Religion, and Wo/men's Struggles for Justice." *DePaul Law Review* 51(4): 1077–1102.

Flannery, Austin, ed. 1998. *Vatican Council II: The Conciliar and Postconciliar Documents*. Northport: Costellow.

Fogel, Susan B, and Lourdes A. Rivera. 2003. "Religious Beliefs and Healthcare Necessities: Can They Coexist!" *Human Rights* 30(3): 8–22.

Fox, Thomas C. 2009. "Vatican Investigates U.S. Women Religious Leadership." *National Catholic Reporter*, April 14. Accessed August 29, 2017. Available at https://www.ncronline.org/news/global-sisters-report/vatican-investigates-us-women-religious-leadership.

French, David A. 2002. *Religious Liberty on Campus*. Philadelphia, PA: Foundation for Individual Rights in Education.

Gaillardetz, Richard. 2010. "Contemporary Religious Life's Creative Fidelity to the Vision of Vatican II" (Speech, Dallas, TX, August 3, 2010), Leadership Conference of Women Religious. Accessed February 1, 2015. Available at https://lcwr.org/calendar/lcwr-assembly-2010.

Goodstein, Laurie. 2012. "Vatican Reprimands a Group of U.S. Nuns and Plans Change." *New York Times*, April 18. Accessed August 29, 2017. Available at http://www.nytimes.com/2012/04/19/us/vatican-reprimands-us-nuns-group.html.

———. 2013. "Pope Says Church Is 'Obsessed' with Gays, Abortion, and Birth Control." *New York Times, Europe*, September 19. Accessed August 29, 2017. Available at http://www.nytimes.com/2013/09/20/world/europe/pope-bluntly-faults-churchs-focus-on-gays-and-abortion.html?pagewanted=all&mcubz=1.

———. 2015. "Vatican Ends Battle with U.S. Catholic Nuns' Group." *New York Times*, April 16. Accessed August 29, 2017. Available at https://www.nytimes.com/2015/04/17/us/catholic-church-ends-takeover-of-leadership-conference-of-women-religious.html.

Goren, Paul, Christopher M. Federico, and Miki L. Kittilson. 2009. "Source Cues, Partisan Identities, and Political Value Expression." *American Journal of Political Science* 53(4): 805–820.

Gray, Mark M. 2015. "The U.S. Catholic Family Demographics: The Second Special Report." *Center for Applied Research in the Apostolate*. Accessed July 8, 2017. Available at http://cara.georgetown.edu/staff/webpages/Catholic%20Families%20Demographics.pdf.

Gray, Mark M., Mary L. Gautier, and Melissa A. Cidade. 2011. "The Changing Face of U.S. Catholic Parishes." *Center for Applied Research in the Apostolate*. Accessed July 8, 2017. Available at http://cara.georgetown.edu/caraservices/parishes%20phase%20one.pdf.

Griffin, Beth. 2012. "Dolan: Natural Law, Not Religious Preferences, Dictates All Life Sacred." *Free Republic*, January 26. Available at http://www.freerepublic.com/focus/f-religion/2838412/posts.

Guth, James L., John C. Green, Corwin E. Smidt, Lyman A. Kellstedt, and Margaret M. Poloma. 1997. *The Bully Pulpit: The Politics of Protestant Clergy*. Lawrence: University of Kansas Press.

Hadden, Jeffrey K. 1969. *The Gathering Storm in Churches*. Garden City, NY: Doubleday.

Hart, Roderick P. 1984. "Systematic Analysis of Political Discourse: The Development of DICTION." In *Political Communication Yearbook: 1984*, ed. K. Sanders, 97–134. Cardbondale, IL: Southern Illinois University Press.

Hart, Roderick P., and Colene J. Lind. 2011. "The Rhetoric of Islamic Activism: A *DICTION* Study." *Dynamics of Asymmetric Conflict* 4(2): 113–125.

Heilman, Samuel. 1992. *Defenders of the Faith: Inside Ultra-Orthodox Jewry.* New York: Shocken.

Hetherington, Marc, and Jonathan Weiler. 2005. "Authoritarian Disposition and Political Choice." Paper presented at the Annual Meeting of the Midwest Political Science Association, Chicago, IL, April 2005.

Heyer-Gray, Z. A. 2000. "Gender and Religious Work." *Sociology of Religion* 61(4): 467–471.

Hiltzik, Michael. 2017. "The GOP's Last-Ditch Obamacare Repeal Bill May Be the Worst One Yet." *Los Angeles Times*, September 18. Accessed July 25, 2017. Available at http://www.latimes.com/business/hiltzik/la-fi-hiltzik-graham-cassidy-20170918-story.html.

Hodges, David R. 2005. "Epistemological Frameworks, Homosexuality, and Religion: How People of Faith Understand the Intersection between Homosexuality and Religion." *National Association of Social Workers* 50(3): 207–218.

Holm, Jean, and John Bowker. 1998. *Women in Religion: Themes in Religious Studies.* London: Pinter.

Holman, Mirya R., and Kristin Shockley. 2017. "Messages from Above: Conflict and Convergence of Messages to the Catholic Voter from the Church Hierarchy." *Politics and Religion* 10:840–861.

Hunter, James D. 1991. *Culture Wars.* New York: Basic Books.

Jelen, Ted G. 1992. "The Clergy and Abortion." *Review of Religious Research* 34(2): 132–151.

———. 2001. "Notes for a Theory of Clergy as Political Leaders." In *Christian Clergy in American Politics*, ed. Sue E. S. Crawford and Laura R. Olson, 15–29. Baltimore, MD: Johns Hopkins University Press.

———. 2003. "Catholic Priests and the Political Order: The Political Behavior of Catholic Pastors." *Journal for the Scientific Study of Religion* 42(4): 591–604.

Jenkins, Jack. 2014. "Catholic Nuns Take on Dark Money in Politics with Nationwide Bus Tour." *Think Progress*, September 18. Accessed July 24, 2017. Available at https://thinkprogress.org/catholic-nuns-take-on-dark-money-in-politics-with-nationwide-bus-tour-95206e263cb2.

———. 2017. "This Catholic Nun Pushed Obamacare through Congress. Now She's Fighting to Save It." *Think Progress*, June 30. Accessed July 23, 2017. Available at https://thinkprogress.org/simone-campbell-health-care-663083582f55/.

Jones-Correa, Michael A., and David L. Leal. 2001. "Political Participation: Does Religion Matter?" *Political Research Quarterly* 54(4): 751–770.

Kam, Cindy D. 2005. "Who Toes the Party Line? Cues, Values, and Individual Differences." *Political Behavior* 27(2): 163–182.

Kathleen, Lyn. 1994. "Power and Influence in State Legislative Policymaking: The Interaction of Gender and Position in Committee Hearing Debates." *American Political Science Review* 88(3): 560–576.

Katzenstein, Mary Fainsod. 1995. "Discursive Politics and Feminist Activism in the Catholic Church." In *Feminist Organizations*, ed. Myra Marx Ferree and Patricia Yancey Martin, 35–52. Philadelphia: Temple University Press.

———. 1998. *Faithful and Fearless: Moving Feminist Protest Inside the Church and Military*. Princeton: Princeton University Press.

King, Ynestra. 1989. "The Ecology of Feminism and the Feminism of Ecology." In *Healing the Wounds: The Power of Ecological Feminism*, ed. Judith Plant, 4–9. Philadelphia, PA: New Society.

Kraybill, Jeanine. 2016. "Evaluating Policy Difference between Male and Female Religious Groups: A Study of Policy Statements by the United States Conference of Catholic Bishops and the Leadership Conference of Women Religious." *Journal of Communication and Religion* 39(3): 76–99.

———. 2017. "Sisters Know Best: Why the Senate Might Want to Listen to Catholic Sisters on Health Care." *Religion in Public: Exploring the Mix of Sacred and Secular*, July 25. Accessed July 25, 2017. Available at https://religioninpublic.blog/2017/07/25/sisters-know-best/.

Kuhns, Elizabeth. 2005. *The Habit: A History of the Clothing of Catholic Nuns*. New York: Doubleday.

Kuklinski, James, and Norman Hurley. 1994. "On Hearing and Interpreting Political Messages: A Cautionary Tale of Citizen Cue-Taking." *Journal of Politics* 56(3): 729–751.

Landers, Richard N. 2011. "Computing Intraclass Correlations (ICC) as Estimates of Interrater Reliability in SPSS." Neoacademic.com, November 16. Accessed January 2, 2016. Available at http://neoacademic.com/2011/11/16/computing-intraclass-correlations-icc-as-estimates-of-interrater-reliability-in-spss/.

Landis, J. R., and G. G. Koch. 1977. "The Measurement of Observer Agreement for Categorical Data." *Biometrics* 33:159–174.

Lau, Richard R., and David P. Redlawsk. 2006. *How Voters Decide: Information Processing during Election Campaigns*. Cambridge: Cambridge University Press.

LCWR (Leadership Conference of Women Religious). 2006. "LCWR National Board Calls for Comprehensive Immigration Policy Reform." Accessed March 3, 2015. Available at https://lcwr.org/media/april-19-2006-lcwr-national-board-calls-comprehensive-immigration-policy-reform.

———. 2015. "Statement of the LCWR Officers on the Congregation for the Doctrine of the Faith's Doctrinal Assessment and Conclusion of the Mandate." Accessed June 1, 2016. Available at https://lcwr.org/media/statement-lcwr-officers-cdf-doctrinal-assessment-and-conclusion-mandate.

———. 2017a. "About LCWR." Accessed July 8, 2017. Available at https://lcwr.org/about.

———. 2017b. "LCWR History." Accessed July 8, 2017. Available at https://lcwr.org/about/history.

———. 2017c. "Links to Religious Congregations and Other Resources." Accessed July 8, 2017. Available at https://lcwr.org/links/organizations.

Leege, David C., Kellstedt, Lyman A., and Wald, Kenneth, D. 1990. "Religion and Politics: A Report on Measures of Religiosity at the 1989 NES

Pilot Study." Paper presented at Annual Meeting of Midwest Political Science Association, Chicago, IL, April 1990.

Lehman, E. C., Jr. 1994. "Gender and Ministry Style: Things Not What They Seem." In *Gender and Religion*, ed. W. H. Swatos Jr., 3–14. New Brunswick: Transaction.

Lenney, Ellen. 1977. "Women's Self Confidence in Achievement Settings." *Psychological Bulletin* 84(1): 1–13.

Levada, William (Cardinal). 2009. "Women Religious Leadership Conference Faces Investigation for Continued 'Problems.'" *Catholic News Agency*, April 18. Accessed August 29, 2017. Available at http://www.catholicnewsagency.com/news/women_religious_leadership_conference_faces_investigation_for_continued_problems/.

Libresco, Leah. September 24, 2015. "Pope Francis Called for More Work from Priest, but 20 Percent of Parishes Don't Have One." Five Thirty Eight. Accessed July 11, 2016. Available at http://fivethirtyeight.com/datalab/pope-francis-us-visit-catholic-priest-shortage/.

Lieblich, Julia. 1992. *Sisters Lives of Devotion and Defiance*. New York: Ballantine Books.

Lipman-Blumen, Jean, and Ann R. Tickamyer. 1975. "Sex Roles in Transition: A Ten-Year Perspective." *Annual Review of Sociology* 1:297–337.

Lummis, Adair T., and Paula Nesbitt. 2000. "Women Clergy Research and the Sociology of Religion." *Sociology of Religion* 61(4): 443–453.

Lupia, Arthur. 1994. "Shortcuts versus Encyclopedias: Information and Voting Behavior in California Insurance Reform Elections." *American Political Science Review* 88(1): 63–76.

Lupia, Arthur, and Mathew D. McCubbins. 1998. *The Democratic Dilemma: Can Citizens Learn What They Need to Know?* Cambridge: Cambridge University Press.

Manson, Jamie. 2016. "It's Time to Be Honest about Pope Francis and Women." *National Catholic Reporter*, May 19. Accessed November 18, 2017. Available at https://www.ncronline.org/blogs/grace-margins/its-time-be-honest-about-pope-francis-and-women.

McCarthy, Justin. 2016. "Americans Still More Trusting in Local over State Government." *Gallup News*, September 19. Accessed November 15, 2017. Available at http://news.gallup.com/poll/195656/americans-trusting-local-state-government.aspx.

McDuff, E. M. 2001. "The Gender Paradox in Work Satisfaction and Protestant Clergy." *Sociology of Religion* 62(1): 1–21.

McElwee, Joshua. 2013. "Pope Francis' LCWR Reaffirmation Leads Sisters to Hard Questions." *National Catholic Reporter*, April 17. Accessed July 8, 2017. Available at https://www.ncronline.org/news/global-sisters-report/pope-francis-lcwr-reaffirmation-leads-sisters-hard-questions.

———. 2015. "Vatican Ends Controversial Three-Year Oversight of U.S. Sisters Leaders." *National Catholic Reporter*, April 16. Accessed March 8, 2017. Available at https://www.ncronline.org/news/vatican/vatican-ends-controversial-three-year-oversight-us-sisters-leaders.

———. 2016. "Full Text of Questions to Francis from Women Religious." *National Catholic Reporter*, May 12. Accessed November 18, 2017. Available at https://www.ncronline.org/blogs/ncr-today/full-text-questions-francis-women-religious.

McGuire, Meredith B. 1997. *Religion: The Social Context*. Belmont, CA: Wadsworth.

McLaughlin, Bryan, and David Wise. 2014. "Cueing God: Religious Cues and Voter Support." *Politics and Religion* 7(2): 366–394.

Merolla, Jennifer, and Elizabeth Zechmeister. 2009. *Democracy at Risk: How Terrorist Threats Affect the Public*. Chicago: University of Chicago Press.

Mondak, Jeffery. 1993a. "Source Cues and Policy Approval: The Cognitive Dynamics of Public Support for the Reagan Agenda." *American Journal of Political Science* 37(1): 186–212.

———. 1993b. "Public Opinion and Heuristic Processing of Source Cues." *Political Behavior* 15(2): 167–192.

Mulligan, Kenneth. 2006. "Pope John Paul II and Catholic Public Opinion toward the Death Penalty and Abortion." *Social Science Quarterly* 87(3): 739–753.

National Catholic Reporter. 2014. "Timeline of Interactions between LCWR, Doctrinal Congregation." May 8. Accessed July 8, 2017. Available at https://www.ncronline.org/blogs/ncr-today/timeline-interactions-between-lcwr-doctrinal-congregation.

Nesbitt. Paula. 1997. *Feminization of the Clergy in America*. New York: Oxford University Press.

NETWORK. 2017. "History." Accessed July 8, 2017. Available at https://networklobby.org/about/history/.

Neuman, Scott. 2012. "Nuns and the Vatican: A Clash Decades in Making." National Public Radio, May 3, 2012. Accessed June 15, 2017. Available at http://www.npr.org/2012/05/03/151943345/nuns-and-the-vatican-a-clash-decades-in-making.

New York Times. 2015. "Pope Francis' Speech to the Bishops of the United States of America." September 23. Accessed August 28, 2017. Available at https://www.nytimes.com/2015/09/24/us/pope-francis-speech-to-the-bishops-of-the-united-states-of-america.html?mcubz=1.

Nicholson, Stephen P. 2011. "Dominating Cues and the Limits of Elite Influence." *Journal of Politics* 73(4): 1165–1177.

NPR (National Public Radio). 2012a. "An American Nun Responds to Vatican Criticism." *Fresh Air*, July 17. Accessed August 29, 2017. Available at http://www.npr.org/2012/07/17/156858223/an-american-nun-responds-to-vatican-condemnation.

———. 2012b. "Bishops Explains Vatican's Criticism of U.S. Nuns." July 25. Accessed July 8, 2017. Available at https://www.npr.org/2012/07/25/157356092/bishop-explains-vaticans-criticism-of-u-s-nuns.

———. 2012c. "Fresh Air Weekend: Bishop Blair, Sister Farrell." July 28. Accessed July 8, 2017. Available at https://www.npr.org/2012/07/28/157441054/fresh-air-weekend-bishop-blair-sister-farrell.

O'Connor, J. 1995. "The Epistemological Significance of Feminist Research in Religion." In *Religion and Gender*, ed. U. King, 45–63. Oxford, UK: Blackwell.

Olson, Laura R. 2000. *Filled with Spirit and Power: Protestant Clergy in American Politics*. Albany: State University of New York Press.

Olson, Laura R., Sue E. S. Crawford, and Melissa M. Deckman. 2005. *Women with a Mission: Religion, Gender, and the Politics of Women Clergy*. Tuscaloosa, AL: University of Alabama Press.

Olson, Laura R., Karen V. Guth, and James L. Guth. 2003. "The Lotto and the Lord: Religious Influences on the Adoption of a Lottery in South Carolina." *Sociology of Religion* 64(1) Spring: 87–110. doi: https://doi.org/10.2307/3712270.

O'Malley, Michael. 2012. "Catholic Rally to Show Support for Nuns amid Vatican Crackdown." Huffington Post, May 30. Accessed July 8, 2017. Available at http://www.huffingtonpost.com/2012/05/30/vatican-crackdown-nuns-catholic-show-support_n_1554238.html.

Owens, Gary. 2008. "Gender Differences in Healthcare Expenditures, Resource Utilization, and Quality of Care." *Journal of Managed Care Pharmacy*14(3): S2. doi: https://doi.org/10.18553/jmcp.2008.14.S6-A.2.

Pew Research Center. 2007. "Changing Faiths: Latinos and the Transformation of American Religion (2006 Hispanic Religion Survey)." Accessed March 16, 2014. Available at http://www.pewhispanic.org/2007/04/25/changing-faiths-latinos-and-the-transformation-of-american-religion-2006-hispanic-religion-survey/.

———. 2016. "Where the Public Stands on Religious Liberty vs. Nondiscrimination." Accessed December 1, 2017. Available at http://assets.pewresearch.org/wp-content/uploads/sites/11/2016/09/Religious-Liberty-full-for-web.pdf.

Pomper, Gerald M. 1972. "From Confusion to Clarity: Issues and American Voters, 1956–1968." *American Political Science Review* 66(2): 415–428.

Quinley, Harold E. 1974. *The Prophetic Clergy: Social Activism among Protestant Ministers*. Hoboken, NJ: John Wiley and Sons.

Rahn, Maike. 2016. "Factor Analysis: A Short Introduction, Part I." The Analysis Factor. Accessed May 15, 2016. Available at https://www.theanalysisfactor.com/factor-analysis-1-introduction/.

Rahn, Wendy. 1993. "The Role of Partisan Stereotypes in Information Processing about Political Candidates." *American Journal of Political Science* 37(2): 472–497.

Reed, Tina. 2015. "Meet the D.C. Nun Praised by President Obama This Week for Her Health Care Work." *Washington Business Journal*, June 12. Accessed July 23, 2017. Available at https://www.bizjournals.com/washington/blog/2015/06/meet-the-d-c-nun-praised-by-president-obama-this.html.

Reese, Thomas. 2016. "The Catholic Story, Conservative v. Progressive." *National Catholic Reporter*, January 7. Accessed November 15, 2017. Available at https://www.ncronline.org/blogs/faith-and-justice/catholic-story-conservative-vs-progressive.

Robinson, Mary. 2004. "Keynote Annual Assembly Address: What Can Religious Bring to a Globalizing World?" (Speech, Fort Worth, TX, August 1, 2004), Leadership Conference of Women Religious. Accessed February 1, 2015. Available at https://lcwr.org/node/4653.

Rosenthal, Cindy S. 1998. *When Women Lead: Integrative Leadership in State Legislatures*. New York: Oxford University Press.

Ross Sammon, Margaret. 2008. "The Politics of the U.S. Catholic Bishops: The Centrality of Abortion." In *Catholics and Politics*, ed. Kristin E. Hayer, Mark J. Rozell, and Michael Genovese, 11–26. Washington, DC: Georgetown University Press.

Sandstrom, Aleksandra. 2016. "Women Relatively Rare in Top Positions of Religious Leadership." Pew Research Center, March 2. Accessed August 20, 2017. Available at http://www.pewresearch.org/fact-tank/2016/03/02/women-relatively-rare-in-top-positions-of-religious-leadership/.

Schlumpf, Heidi. 2011. "Femme Fidele: How Women Who Work for the Church Keep the Faith." *U.S. Catholic* 76(1): 12–17.

———. 2015. "The Inevitable Question for Women: To Stay or Go?" *National Catholic Reporter*, December 3. Accessed November 13, 2017. Available at https://www.ncronline.org/news/people/inevitable-question-women-stay-or-go.

Schneider, Anne, and Helen Ingram. 1993. "Social Construction of Target Populations: Implications for Politics and Policy Author(s)." *American Political Science Review* 87(2): 334–347.

Seaman, Kristopher. 2013. "Why Did the Second Vatican Council Occur?" Pastoralliturgy.org. Accessed July 8, 2017. Available at http://www.pastoralliturgy.org/resources/1301ReproRsrc.pdf.

Sell, Jane, W. I. Griffith, and Rick K. Wilson. 1993. "Are Women More Cooperative Than Men in Social Dilemmas?" *Social Psychology Quarterly* 56(3): 211–222.

Sered, Susan. 1997. "Women and Religious Change in Israel: Rebellion or Revolution." *Sociology of Religion* 58(1): 1–24.

Shapiro, Robert Y., and Harpreet Mahajan. 1986. "Gender Differences in Policy Preferences: A Summary of Trends from the 1960s to the 1980s." *Public Opinion Quarterly* 50(1): 42–61.

Siegel, Jonas. 2012. "Religious Views on Climate Change Mitigation." Center for International and Security Studies at Maryland." Accessed December 1, 2012. Available at http://www.cissm.umd.edu/publications/religious-views-climate-change-mitigation-0.

Smidt, Corwin E., ed. 2004. *Pulpit and Politics: Clergy in American Politics at the Advent of the Millennium*. Waco, TX: Baylor University Press.

Smidt, Corwin E., Kevin R. den Dulk, James M. Penning, Stephen V. Monsma, and Douglas L. Koopman. 2008. *Pews, Prayers and Participation: Religion and Civic Responsibility in America*. Washington, DC: Georgetown University Press.

Smidt, Corwin E., and Brian Schaap. 2009. "Public Worship and Public Engagement: Pastoral Cues within the Context of Worship Services." *Religious Research Association* 50(4): 441–462.

Smith, Gregory Allen. 2008. *Politics in the Parish: The Political Influence of Catholic Priests*. Washington, DC: Georgetown University Press.

Snarr, Melissa C. 2009. "Religion, Race, and Bridge Building in Economic Justice Coalitions." *Journal of Labor and Society* 12(1): 73–95.

Stalp, Marybeth C., and Bill Winders. 2002. "Power in the Margins: Gendered Organizational Effects on Religious Activism." *Religious Research Association* 2(1) 41–60.

Stenner, Karen. 2005. *The Authoritarian Dynamic*. Cambridge: Cambridge University Press.

Sunshine, Edward R. 1989. "The Primacy of Abortion in the Moral Rhetoric of U.S. Catholic Bishops." *Annual of the Society of Christian Ethics* 9:167–186.

Thomas, Susan. 1997. "Why Gender Matters: The Perceptions of Women Officeholders." *Women and Politics* 17(1): 27–53.

Thompson, Edward H., Jr. 1991. "Beneath the Status Characteristic: Gender Variations in Religiousness." *Journal for the Scientific Study of Religion* 30(4): 381–394.

Thompson, Margaret. 1986. "Discovering Foremothers: Sisters, Society, and the American Catholic Experience." *U.S. Catholic Historian* 5:273–290.

USCCB (United States Conference of Catholic Bishops). 1986. *Economic Justice for All: Pastoral Letter on Catholic Social Teaching and the U.S. Economy.* Accessed February 1, 2015. Available at http://www.usccb.org/upload/economic_justice_for_all.pdf.

———. 2000. "Welcoming the Stranger among Us: Unity in Diversity." Accessed February 1, 2015. Available at http://www.usccb.org/issues-and-action/cultural-diversity/pastoral-care-of-migrants-refugees-and-travelers/resources/welcoming-the-stranger-among-us-unity-in-diversity.cfm.

———. 2002. "A Place at the Table." Accessed February 1, 2015. Available at http://www.usccb.org/issues-and-action/human-life-and-dignity/poverty/place-at-the-table.cfm.

———. 2005. "A Culture of Life or Death." Accessed June 1, 2016. Available at http://www.usccb.org/issues-and-action/human-life-and-dignity/death-penalty-capital-punishment/upload/penaltyofdeath.pdf.

———. 2006. *Ministering to People with Homosexual Inclinations.* Accessed February 1, 2015. Available at http://www.usccb.org/issues-and-action/human-life-and-dignity/homosexuality/upload/minstry-persons-homosexual-inclination-2006.pdf.

———. 2007. *Forming Conscience for Faithful Citizenship, a Call to Political Responsibility.* Accessed June 1, 2016. Available at http://www.usccb.org/issues-and-action/faithful-citizenship/upload/forming-consciences-for-faithful-citizenship.pdf.

———. 2009a. "Marriage: Love and Life in the Divine Plan." Accessed May 15, 2016. Available at http://www.usccb.org/upload/marriage-love-life-divine-plan-2009.pdf.

———. 2009b. "Making Healthcare Reform Abortion Neutral: What Is the Legal Status Quo on Abortion?" Accessed May 15, 2016. Available at http://www.usccb.org/issues-and-action/human-life-and-dignity/health-care/upload/health-care-backgrounder-abortion-2009-07-17.pdf.

———. 2010a. "Catholic Social Teaching Scripture Guide." Accessed November 27, 2017. Available at http://www.usccb.org/beliefs-and-teachings/how-we-teach/catholic-education/campus-ministry/tools-for-action/upload/cst-scripture-guide-donna-update-matt2.pdf.

———. 2010b. "Human Life and Dignity." Accessed February 1, 2015. Available at http://www.usccb.org/issues-and-action/human-life-and-dignity/index.cfm.

———. 2011. "Affordable Housing and the National Housing Trust Fund." Accessed May 15, 2016. Available at http://usccb.org/issues-and-action/human-life-and-dignity/housing-homelessness/affordable-housing-and-the-national-housing-trust-fund.cfm.

———. 2012a. "March 14 Statement on Religious Freedom and HHS Mandate." Accessed July 8, 2017. Available at http://www.usccb.org/issues-and-action/religious-liberty/march-14-statement-on-religious-freedom-and-hhs-mandate.cfm.

———. 2012b. "Vatican Names Archbishop Sartain to Lead Renewal of LCWR." News Releases. Accessed July 8, 2017. Available at http://www.usccb.org/news/2012/12-062e.cfm.

———. 2012c. "Federal Budget: Advocating a Circle of Protection." Accessed July 8, 2017. Available at http://www.usccb.org/about/justice-peace-and-human-development/catholic-social-ministry-gathering/upload/Federal-budget-backgrounder-2012.pdf

———. 2017a. "About USCCB." Accessed July 8, 2017. Available at http://www.usccb.org/about/.

———. 2017b. "Discrimination against Catholic Adoption Services." Accessed August 29, 2017. Available at http://www.usccb.org/issues-and-action/religious-liberty/discrimination-against-catholic-adoption-services.cfm.

Vatican. 1965a. *Christus Dominus*. Accessed July 8, 2017. Available at http://www.vatican.va/archive/hist_councils/ii_vatican_council/documents/vat-ii_decree_19651028_christus-dominus_en.html.

———. 1965b. *Perfectae Caritatis*. Accessed July 8, 2017. Available at http://www.vatican.va/archive/hist_councils/ii_vatican_council/documents/vat-ii_decree_19651028_perfectae-caritatis_en.html.

———. 1988. "Apostolic Constitution." Accessed July 8, 2017. Available at http://w2.vatican.va/content/john-paul-ii/en/apost_constitutions/documents/hf_jp-ii_apc_19880628_pastor-bonus-index.html.

———. 1994. "Ordinatio Sacerdotalis." Accessed August 14, 2017. Available at https://w2.vatican.va/content/john-paul-ii/en/apost_letters/1994/documents/hf_jp-ii_apl_19940522_ordinatio-sacerdotalis.html.

———. 2000. "Dominus Iesus." Accessed July 8, 2017. Available at http://www.vatican.va/roman_curia/congregations/cfaith/documents/rc_con_cfaith_doc_20000806_dominus-iesus_en.html.

———. 2009. "Caritas in Veritate." Accessed November 15, 2017. Available at http://w2.vatican.va/content/benedict-xvi/en/encyclicals/documents/hf_ben-xvi_enc_20090629_caritas-in-veritate.html.

Vatican Congregation for the Doctrine of Faith. 2012. "Doctrinal Assessment of the Leadership Conference of Women Religious." Accessed June 1, 2016. Available at http://www.usccb.org/upload/Doctrinal_Assessment_Leadership_Conference_Women_Religious.pdf.

"Vatican Orders Doctrinal Assessment of Group Representing U.S. Nuns." 2012. *Catholic Review*, January 19. Accessed August 29, 2017. http://www.archbalt.org/vatican-orders-doctrinal-assessment-of-group-representing-us-nuns/.

Vatican Radio. 2016. "Vatican Commission on Female Diaconate Holds First Meeting." November 25. Accessed July 25, 2017. Available at http://en.radiovaticana.va/news/2016/11/25/vatican_commission_on_female_diaconate_holds_first_meeting/1274887.

Waggoner, Tim. 2008. "Over 80 Bishops Say Abortion/Life Issues Defining Issues of Election." Life Sites, October 27. Accessed November 15, 2017. Available at https://www.lifesitenews.com/news/over-80-bishops-say-abortion-life-issues-defining-issues-of-election.

Wald, Kenneth. 1992. "Religious Elites and Public Opinion: The Impact of the Bishops' Peace Pastoral." *Review of Politics* 54(1): 112–143.

Wallace, Ruth A. 1988. "Catholic Women and the Creation of a New Social Reality." *Gender and Society* 2(1): 24–38.

Warner, Michael. 1995. *Changing Witness Catholic Bishops and Public Policy*, 1917–1994. Grand Rapids, MI: Eerdmans.

Warren, Karen J., and Jim Cheney. 1991. "Ecological Feminism and Ecosystem Ecology." *Hypatia* 6(1): 179–197.

Watling, Tony. 2002. "'Leadership' or 'Dialogue'? Women, Authority and Religious Change in a Netherlands Community." *Sociology of Religion* 63(4): 515–538.

Welch, Michelle R., David C. Leege, Kenneth D. Walt, and Lyman A. Kellstedt. 1993. "Are the Sheep Hearing the Shepherds? Cue Perceptions, Congregational Responses, and Political Communication Processes," In *Rediscovering the Religious Factor in American Politics*, ed. David C. Leege and Lyman Kellstedt, 235–254. New York: M. E. Sharp.

Wilcox, Clyde, and Ted G. Jelen. 2003. "Causes and Consequences of Public Attitudes toward Abortion: A Review and Research Agenda." Accessed July 24, 2017. Available at http://faculty.georgetown.edu/wilcoxc/Abortion.pdf.

Wilcox, Clyde, and Lee Sigelman. 2001. "Political Mobilization in the Pews: Religious Contacting and Electoral Turnout." *Social Science Quarterly* 82(3): 524–535. doi: https://doi.org/10.1111/0038-4941.00040.

The Williams Institute. 2009. "Best Practices for Asking Questions about Sexual Orientation on Surveys." Accessed May 1, 2014. Available at https://williamsinstitute.law.ucla.edu/wp content/uploads/SMART-FINAL-Nov-2009.pdf.

Wittberg, Patricia. 1989. "Non-ordained Workers in the Catholic Church: Power and Mobility among American Nuns." *Journal for the Scientific Study of Religion* 28(2): 148–161.

Wittman, Donald A. 1995. *The Myth of Democratic Failure: Why Political Institutions Are Efficient.* Chicago: University of Chicago Press.

Zaller, John R. 1992. *The Nature and Origins of Mass Opinion.* Cambridge: Cambridge University Press.

Zollman, Mary Ann. 2003. "Annual Assembly Presidential Address: Tending the Holy through the Power of Sisterhood." (Speech, Detroit, MI, August 22, 2003), Leadership Conference of Women Religious. Accessed March 13, 2013. Available at https://lcwr.org/presidential-address-mary-ann-zollmann-bvm.

Index

Jeanine E. Kraybill is an Assistant Professor in the Department of Political Science at California State University, Bakersfield. She is the editor and contributing author of *Unconventional, Partisan, and Polarizing Rhetoric: How the 2016 Election Shaped the Way Candidates Strategize, Engage, and Communicate*. Her work has been featured in *Fieldwork in Religion* and the *Journal of Communication and Religion*, as well as *Oxford's Encyclopedia for Religion and Politics.*